Healing with Heart

INSPIRATIONS FOR HEALTH CARE PROFESSIONALS

MARTIN HELLDORFER, D.MIN. AND TERRI MOSS

D1025981

MOSS COMMUNICATIONS

Moss Communications
P.O. Box 344
Orinda, CA 94563
Tel: (925)377-5288
Fax: (925)377-5244
mosscomm@mindspring.com

ORDERING INFORMATION

Special discounts are available for bulk purchases. Please contact Moss Communications for more information.

Moss Communications books are printed using paper that has been manufactured by environmentally responsible processes, when available. This may include using trees grown in sustainable forests and incorporating recycled paper. This book has been printed using soy-based ink.

Designed by Nicole Watson, Pensé Design, 875 4th St. San Rafael, CA www.pensedesign.com
Printed in the U.S.A. by Hartford Media, Berkeley, CA. www.hartfordmedia.com.

Library of Congress Cataloguing-in-Publication Data
Library of Congress Control Number: 2007903780
Helldorfer, Martin
Moss, Terri
Healing with Heart, Inspirations for Health Care Professionals/by Martin Helldorfer and Terri Moss
p. cm.
ISBN 13: 978-0-615-14388-0

DEDICATED TO THOSE WHO...

... are the hidden saints, who inspire us.

...risk all, in order to excel in patient care.

...find protected time for reflection in the midst of busy days.

...are, above all, a healing presence to patients and caregivers alike.

THANK YOU

"This is a remarkable book, one that everyone working in health care should make a part of their day because it will inspire and enrich their work experience. The wise and insightful reflections will remind them of why they went into this field in the first place and chose to expose themselves to its challenges. Marty's rich wisdom and firsthand knowledge of in-the-trenches health care will grab readers and inspire them to live up to their highest potential. This is a win-win proposition for everyone: employees, administrators and patients. I believe it deserves a place on everyone's desk as a gentle reminder that our strength, courage and individual talents really do matter."

Dean Edell, M.D.

Nationally-syndicated television and radio talk show host
Best Selling Author

∿

"*Healing with Heart* is a must-read for all health care employees. It provides encouragement and inspirational support for novice nurses as well as experts who have been in the field for years. This captivating handbook reminds us of the sacredness of our profession and the intricate beauty and necessity of working together as a team. This book will resonate throughout any health care organization; for those providing direct patient care as well as those supporting them. Senior executives, accountants, surgeons, nurses, admitting clerks, janitors and volunteers will all see the value of their unique contributions to our common goal of providing safe, quality care to our patients and their families."

Anne M. Hirsch, D.N.S., A.R.N.P.

Interim Dean & Professor
Washington State University Intercollegiate College of Nursing

"THE WEEKLY THOUGHT FROM MISSION [THE EMAILS THAT ARE THE BASIS FOR *Healing with Heart*] IS THE MOST UNIQUE FORM OF COMMUNICATION THAT I HAVE EVER SEEN DURING ALMOST THIRTY YEARS OF WORKING IN HOSPITALS. THE MEANING OF MISSION OR HOW THE SPIRIT OF ONE'S MISSION CONNECTS WITH THE ORGANIZATION AS A WHOLE, IS OFTEN LACKING OR MISUNDERSTOOD. MARTY HELLDORFER HAS PERFECTED AN ENLIGHTENING WAY TO MAKE THIS CONNECTION REAL, THUS TRULY BRINGING MISSION TO LIFE, AND FOR THAT HE IS TO BE CONGRATULATED."

Les Hirsch
President and Chief Executive Officer
Touro Infirmary, New Orleans, LA

☙

"I HAVE READ MARTY'S REFLECTIONS [THOUGHT FROM MISSION, THE BASIS FOR *Healing with Heart*] WEEKLY FOR THE PAST FIVE YEARS AND HAVE BEEN AMAZED BY HIS CREATIVITY. . . AND HIS ABILITY TO ADDRESS ISSUES THAT ARE PERTINENT TO THE AVERAGE EMPLOYEE AND OTHER WEEKS TO PHYSICIANS AND CLINICIANS. HE CONSISTENTLY HIGHLIGHTS THE DIGNITY OF THE PERSON AND HOW ALL OF US, NO MATTER OUR SOCIO-ECONOMIC OR EDUCATIONAL LEVEL, MUST WRESTLE WITH LIFE, DEATH, ILLNESS, SURPRISE TRAUMATIC EVENTS AND BASIC RESPECT FOR ONE ANOTHER. I OFTEN FORWARDED HIS REFLECTIONS TO OUR PALLIATIVE CARE AND HOSPICE CLINICIANS WHO APPRECIATED HIS ABILITY TO CONNECT ULTIMATE LIFE ISSUES WITH BASIC DAY-TO-DAY LIVING. THEY OFTEN COMMENTED ON HOW HELPFUL IT WAS TO BE REMINDED OF THE IMPORTANCE OF CARING FOR ONE ANOTHER. I WELCOME THIS BOOK, AS WILL OTHERS. THIS IS THE KIND OF BOOK I WOULD LIKE TO RECEIVE AS A GIFT!"

John Perring-Mulligan, Ph.D.
SVP Mission Services
Affinity Health System, Menasha, WI

"WE ARE OFTEN GUILTY OF LOOKING BUT NOT REALLY SEEING. THROUGH STORIES DRAWN FROM EVERYDAY LIFE, WORK AND RELATIONSHIPS, MARTIN GIVES US REASON TO TAKE NOTICE. HIS GENTLE YET PROVOCATIVE AFFIRMATIONS CALL THOSE WHO STRIVE TO HEAL OTHERS TO SEE THEMSELVES AND THOSE AROUND THEM WITH RENEWED CLARITY, INSIGHT, AND APPRECIATION. THIS COMPILATION OF HIS MESSAGES IS TRULY A GIFT TO THOSE WHO GIVE SO MUCH."

Dorothy Horrell, Ph.D.
Executive Director
Bonfils-Stanton Foundation

∽◎∾

"MARTIN HELLDORFER AND TERRI MOSS REMIND US THAT HEALTH CARE IS MORE THAN A SINGLE, HIGHLY EDUCATED, WELL TRAINED INDIVIDUAL WORKING HARD TO ALLEVIATE SUFFERING. NO, THEY TELL US, HEALTH CARE—IN ANY SETTING— IS A COMMUNITY ENTERPRISE, ONE, WHICH EXTENDS FROM THE BOILER ROOM TO THE SURGICAL SUITE. HELLDORFER AND MOSS CHALLENGE US TO UNDERSTAND THE "CARE" IN HEALTH CARE AS INTEREST, CONCERN, AND SOLICITUDE EXTENDED TO PATIENT, COLLEAGUE AND CO-WORKER.

THROUGH A SERIES OF THOUGHTFUL REFLECTIONS AND DAILY EXERCISES, WE ARE CHALLENGED TO DEEPEN OUR PROFESSIONAL LIVES BY ENVISIONING OUR WORK AS MORE THAN THE ORGANIZING, MANAGING, AND EFFICIENT CONTROL OF A HEALTH CARE DELIVERY SYSTEM. WE ARE CHALLENGED TO DEEPEN THE PERSON WE BRING TO OUR PROFESSION. WE ARE INVITED TO AWAKEN OUR PASSION FOR OUR WORK BY IMAGINING OUR SKILL AS A GIFT; A GIFT WE PUT AT THE DISPOSAL OF OTHERS.

WE ARE INVITED TO IMAGINE CURE OF A SICK BODY AS THE HEALING— THE MAKING WHOLE—OF BODY, MIND, AND SPIRIT.

By helping us to awaken to the vulnerability of self—a self often stretched too far—Helldorfer and Moss show us how to take stock of our own needs and draw upon the energy of the health care community, a community of dedicated healers. Helldorfer and Moss show us the small ways in which we can connect with others and grow big as individuals, individuals who are part of a larger community; a community, which, through a variety of activities, is dedicated to the cure of the patient. Helldorfer and Moss guide us toward the daily practice of small activities which lift others up in an attitude of reverence and respect, and transform "cure" into a corporate, professional activity that lovingly and passionately heals people who are suffering."

Thomas J. Tyrrell, Ph.D.

Pastoral Counseling Center of Santa Fe, New Mexico

About This Book

Healing with Heart is based on weekly inspirational emails, *Thoughts from Mission*, that Dr. Helldorfer has been writing for the past six years to the employees, physicians and volunteers of Exempla Healthcare, a multi-hospital system in the Denver, Colorado area. His training in psychology, experience as a health care executive, and his life as a de la Salle monk infuse his writings with a gentle, judgment-free, and relentlessly optimistic perspective. As he walks the halls of the hospitals, medical centers and offices, talks to people and observes the unfolding of everyday life, he has recorded his reflections, *Thoughts from Mission*, and now *Healing with Heart*. When you see "I" mentioned in this book, it is referring to Marty and to his experiences within the hospitals.

Pick Up This Book When....

- You need an upbeat dose of inner reality.
- You want to begin your day remembering that life is bigger than the pressures around you.
- You want to start your day over with a realigned perspective.
- You have that inner ache that says that you want more out of your work life.
- You need an encouraging nudge to stretch and try something new.
- You feel alone and want to reconnect with your humanity and the humanity of others.
- You need a friend to tell you that what you do counts and that you are in the right place to do great things.

We hope this book becomes a reliable friend that you can turn to for encouragement, and as a reminder of the invaluable role you play in so many lives.

Table of Contents

Forward

Within health care, the mission of fostering healing and health to the people and communities we serve, is often lost in our effort to bring the best of medical technology to our patients, create the best working environment for our hospital and medical staff, and at the same time, manage the vital signs of our hospitals. As a result, it becomes easy to believe that budgets, systems, and managerial controls should be the central theme of our leadership. This is especially true at a time when we are challenged by higher costs, lower reimbursement, and a health care market that, on the surface does not seem to value the spiritual side of healing and health. Consequently, we can lose our way as leaders, believing that the business we are in is more important than the sacred work we do.

I have known Martin Helldorfer for six years. When we met, he was hired as our mission leader. In this short time, Martin has changed my sense of what is important in terms of leadership, both with his presence and with his weekly *Thoughts from Mission*.

His weekly commentary reminds us that we are human beings, not human doings: that being fully present with our patients and with each other is the most important step in bringing a healing presence to those we serve. Martin also reminds us that we are never alone in what concerns us; that indeed we are a community of people who share the same anxieties and sense of scarcity, and a common desire to serve those in need. With this realization, we find strength in each other and in the desire to overcome the barriers that are before us.

Healing with Heart is a compilation of thoughts, beliefs, reflections and stories that help us bring a sense of compassion, wonder, and love into the workplace. They are a source of inspiration as we address the challenges of the day. They also help us to be fully present to those who entrust us with their care.

Martin and his writings have been a true gift to me and to the Exempla family. I expect that they will be the same for you.

Jeffrey Selberg
President and CEO
Exempla Healthcare

～⊚～

WE ARE CHANGED BY TRAGEDY AND DEATH. WHILE THESE EVENTS AWAKEN FEELINGS OF HELPLESSNESS, WE KNOW THAT WE ARE NOT. WE MUST BE MINDFUL OF THE GOODNESS OF LIFE AND OF EACH HUMAN BEING BY MAKING SURE THAT OUR PERSONAL THOUGHTS, DREAMS, ENERGIES AND ACTIONS ALWAYS NURTURE THE HUMANITY WE SHARE.

WORLDWIDE VIOLENCE HAS RAISED OUR FEARS, BUT IT HAS ALSO REAWAKENED OUR APPRECIATION OF LIFE AND OF ONE ANOTHER. NOW IS THE TIME TO REFLECT, IF ONLY FOR A FEW MOMENTS, ON WHAT WE ARE DOING AND HOW WE ARE DOING IT. WHEN WE DO, IT IS EASIER TO RETURN TO WORK WITH PERSPECTIVE, RENEWED ENERGY, AND COMMITMENT. EVERY PATIENT AND EACH COLLEAGUE DESERVES THIS OF US.

TAKE A MOMENT TO REFLECT THAT OUR LIVES REST ON THE LIVES OF OTHERS. SLOW DOWN ENOUGH TO RECOGNIZE YOUR RESPONSIBILITY TO HELP CREATE AND BETTER OUR GOD-GIVEN WORLD.

Introduction

Each week, for the past six years, I have written a *Thought From Mission* to the employees and physicians of Exempla Healthcare. Every reflection has been tied to a real-life event in the lives of these remarkable professionals. Each was written for the purpose of helping the busy professional recognize the value of their work. These are not motivational snippets or how-to essays. Rather, they are simply the unwrapping of everyday experiences to reflect on their beauty, meaning and value. Please welcome them as you would a guest into your home.

Almost every patient who enters a hospital, medical office, or treatment center, has lost something. What they have lost, or fear they may have lost, is their health. That is an incredibly unsettling event that places patients in a particularly uncomfortable and vulnerable position. They know, in a way that many do not, that life is precious.

When working within health care, it is a challenge to remember that a hospital or medical office is a space where love is expressed in a particularly unique way. Our work, within the world of technology, is to create a healing environment for those entrusted to our care. That is an extraordinary responsibility.

The people working within health care tend to be busy and eminently practical people. We do not have a lot of time for theorizing. Finding moments to reflect on how-we-do what-we-do is difficult enough; having time to read is even more of a challenge. We hope that these short essays will help all of us recognize the value of what we are about. It is work that is often viewed as a job, frequently seen as ordinary. It is best seen, however, as a calling, with the sacred thinly veiled from view.

Martin C. Helldorfer

Acknowledgments

MARTIN HELLDORFER

Often, I have been asked "where do you get those thoughts, week after week?" There is only one place of which I am aware. They come from the women and men with whom I work.

Have you ever been to the theater or to a ball game and noticed fans clamoring to meet with the rich and famous? Who is not a little boastful after having shaken hands or of having a photo taken with a celebrity?

For the past six years, I have rubbed shoulders with extraordinary individuals of inestimable value. They have worked in the cellars of the medical centers, at the bedside of patients, in hidden cubicles of windowless office buildings, in EDs and ORs, and innumerable physician offices. I have no need to look for greatness. I have found it among my colleagues. You are the ones to be acknowledged.

If you find these words helpful, they are yours. If they are not helpful, I ask for your pardon for I have been unable to express the goodness I have found in you.

On an entirely different note, this book would never have seen the light of day without the inspiration, passion, dedication, stick-to-itiveness, and downright doggedness of Terri Moss. She is gifted and delightful. No author could have a better friend.

TERRI MOSS

Healing with Heart has been a great journey for me. It started with a bad case of work burnout and a flame of passion that was re-ignited when I was introduced to Marty Helldorfer's writings. The flame has been burning ever since, guiding me, propelling me to publish this book.

I have had many supporters and angels along the way. Thanks to Amanita Rosenbush, a talented editor who took this material and added depth, polish and texture with a degree of dedication and thoughtfulness that was inspiring. Our sessions were filled with debates about spirituality and many trips to the synonym finder.

Many thanks to my women friends for their never-ending belief in me, and for holding up the signs that pointed the way; to Susan and Aaron for a last-minute read and invaluable second opinion; and to my friends in health care, whose opinions and encouragement kept me going. Thank you also to my creative and loyal production team of Nicole Watson, Pensé Design, for your beautiful work, and to Chet Shaw at Hartford Media, for your optimism and willingness to find a way to make this book happen.

Healing with Heart would not have been possible without my dear cousin Evonne, who juiced the spark by introducing me to Marty, and who has held my hand the whole way. Your creativity and love are awe-inspiring. And, I am deeply grateful for my husband, Jack, who has steadfastly supported me and trusted my vision. Your love is my rock.

And finally, to my wise and generous co-author, Marty, whose words inspired me from the moment I read them. They pulled me out of a malaise of cynicism and despair, and suggested that reflection, love, and sacredness have a valid place at work. Thank you for trusting me to shape your thoughts into *Healing with Heart*, so they can expand their reach and lift others to new levels of healing. You are a blessing in my life, and in the lives of countless others.

*H*ealing *Presence*

All of us are in need of healing, whether we are in a hospital or not. On an emotional level, past conflicts and lost dreams lodge in our memory and subtly find their way into our lives. Kind words, an understanding glance, a favor offered, and honest conversations go a long way to healing the wounds we carry.

Bringing a healing presence to one another doesn't require special training or expertise. On the contrary, we are a healing presence to one another in ordinary ways that are easy to overlook.

- When a nurse notices and lingers with a patient who is fearful, he is a healing presence.
- When a technically proficient physician remembers that she is a physician-healer, as well as a physician-scientist, the door to healing is opened.
- When an office assistant offers to cover for a colleague in need, even before being asked, there is healing.
- When a patient representative listens attentively and turns to help a complaining family member, families are healed.
- When a supervisor genuinely makes time to acknowledge, support, and lead their colleagues, there is healing in the relationships.

If we fail as a healing presence, it is simply because we have forgotten that all of us are in need of healing and that there is none without recognizing how important we are to one another.

A CEO explained being a "healing presence" to his board in this way:

"Creating a healing presence is a way of extending ourselves compassionately to those we serve. Our patients, our staff, and our community are in need of it. Within health care it has been buried too deep for too long. Each of us, regardless of title, position, or role, has the opportunity to be a healing presence. It involves placing our patients' needs first, not our own. This is what will bring the magic back into health care."

I will look for ways to listen and support the people I come in contact with today. I will remember to be a conscious, healing presence in all that I do.

Taking a "Protected Time" to Reflect

A speaker from one of the nation's most prestigious medical centers once casually remarked that a significant barrier standing in the way of offering the highest quality of patient care is not being able to "protect time for reflection."

What does this mean? It means we must acknowledge the need to separate from our every day world for private time that is dedicated to uninterrupted, focused thought—and creating that opportunity for ourselves regularly. When we work in a frenzied manner, it hinders the quality of care. Taking time for reflection is fragile and needs to be protected.

How would our work place be different if we allowed time for reflection? Patient floors and our offices would be increasingly more relaxed places to work. There would be time during meetings to reflect on what we were doing, where we were going, and how we were going to get there. We would be encouraged to stand back and think creatively about how to get the work done in our patients' best interests. We would likely share more of our thoughts and experiences with our colleagues.

With protected time for reflection, we would work more calmly, increase our awareness and trust our feelings.

Is it possible to set up this culture in hospitals, treatment centers and offices? Many would say, "Are you kidding me? There is already too much to do and too many demands on us." This belief is persuasive, yet self-defeating. It keeps us from creating a balanced life. By believing this, we lose perspective; every task becomes one more thing to do in an already hectic day. Discouragement follows.

We can control and influence the way we work and shape the work place by making small but significant changes. Here are a few suggestions:

- Arrive for work fifteen minutes early.
- Sit down with a cup of coffee and think about how to go about what needs to be done.
- Say to yourself: There are four things I must finish today. I know that I will only be able to do three of them (not an unfamiliar situation for many clinicians). These are the three I choose to do.
- Take a break now and again during the course of a workday. If we do not take it, we have a hint that we have fallen into the trap of thinking that we are helpless and that others are controlling our lives.

Something curious happens when we take protected time—our pace slows. Curiously, we make better decisions, are more effective, and less overwhelmed. The challenge is to take responsibility for our lives, something easier said than done.

Today, I will slow down and reflect on my work and the opportunities that await me. I will protect the time I need to reflect so that I may bring a new thoughtfulness to my work. I will encourage others to do the same.

$\mathcal{D}$oing What We Love

Ted, the executive who works in the office next to mine, arrives well before 7 a.m., sometimes earlier, and the first thing he does is to make coffee for all of us. I'm no slacker when it comes to working long hours, but he's still in the office when I leave. Picture someone who is pleasant, good-natured and competent, who has a quietly infectious personality, and you will begin to describe Ted. I wish everyone had the opportunity to work beside this man.

Why do some people come early and stay late? Why do certain employees have such a pleasant attitude toward their coworkers, while others are testy or demanding? Why are some easy with what the day brings, while others are bothered by the slightest task and irritated with any question that is asked of them? The difference lies in whether the person is just clocking in hours to pick up a paycheck or whether he is what researchers call a "vocation-loving" individual.

While they represent a small percentage of the workforce, vocation-loving people probably make up more of the workforce than we imagine. They are relaxed in the busyness of the day's activities, they can keep their perspective when everyone around is losing theirs, they enjoy their vacations yet don't curse the day they return to work. Whenever they talk about their work, they make it sound fun, interesting and meaningful. Yet as devoted as these people are to their job, they are not driven as if their whole identity were wrapped up in it. They are balanced enough that they still see themselves as fathers, mothers, friends and citizens, too.

You might say, "Easy for him, he's not on the floor all day with sick patients. He has a no-pressure job!" You would be wrong. While it's true that Ted doesn't work directly with patients, you can find people like him working in any position. They could be social workers, plumbers, physicians, chefs, or nurses. Their attitude has nothing to do with the job itself. What they possess that's unique is an inner love and a sense of mission for the work itself. Vocation-loving individuals are the people who want to do what they have to do. Many of us are what researchers call "ordinary." That is, when we go to work, we feel that we're there to do what we have to do. When we can do what we want, we call it leisure time. Vocation-loving individuals don't make that separation.

When a job becomes a vocation, time moves easily from work to play. Who are these people in your place of work and how is your own humanity touched by them?

Today, I will look around and notice my vocation-loving colleagues. I will thank them for the positive influence they have on my work and I will strive to turn my work into my passion. If I am a vocation-loving person, I will continue to be grateful for the gift I've been given—to love the work I do.

Committing to Excellence

Sunday is the Super Bowl. Those who love the game will be glued to the TV. Everyone else must wonder what the attraction is to kicking a ball down a field. The appeal is not just the sport, but also the drama. It is an opportunity to be recognized as the best, and that is measured by winning.

Hospitals, believe it or not, share some similarities with football. Obviously, our work isn't about blocking and tackling to a goal line. Yet, there are some common features. All of us have the inner desire to excel. We want to defeat heart disease, avoidable cancers and diabetes. We want to reduce infant mortality and birth defects. We are combating sky-rocketing medical costs, careless use of resources and poor communications among teams and departments. And, we are competing against ourselves to reduce medical errors, save lives, improve safety, and make our facilities more efficient, clean, and healthy places to work and serve those entrusted to our care.

World-class athletes build their lives around a dream. It is not unusual to hear them say that they go to the gym before work and return soon after work. They watch what they eat and limit any activities that distract them from their training. Their bodies change accordingly. Swimmers develop incredible upper body strength. Shot putters seem Herculean. Sprinters are lean and muscular. They are all thoroughly focused.

We are not world-class athletes, yet we do have a desire to become the best at what we do. We have the same commitment to excellence.

Some will say this analogy is a stretch. Football is about aggressive competition, inflated egos, and money. Hospitals are about care, science, and healing...and yes, money. Yet beneath both is the same human desire to excel. Both efforts take commitment to a worthy goal. Both require courage, fortitude, a full heart and a clear mind. We are talking about an inward drive, a hunger to make a difference. Imagine what we could accomplish if we brought the energy needed to win a championship to the care of patients.

What does commitment look like in a medical facility? It is the radiologist who is extraordinarily careful, who takes a second and third look at a film and notices something that no one else has seen. It is the lab technician who carefully checks her work or the food service worker who suggests an array of low-fat dishes in the cafeteria. It is the nurse who consistently and conscientiously makes the effort to ensure clear lines of communications among all team members involved in her patient's care. It is the resident who brings fresh eyes to a diagnosis, the plumber who works overtime to find a corroded pipe before it bursts, the PBX operator who makes a special effort to be pleasant even when the caller is not, and the IT technician who keeps her knowledge, skills, and our equipment updated so she can help us when there is a problem. It is the medical team who directs patients to make healthier lifestyle choices, and the department managers who find more efficient ways to run their departments while supporting the goal of patient safety. There are as many ways to excel as there are employees. Everyone contributes to the task of becoming the best.

Am I committed to excel in my work? As an individual contributor and in my role as a team player, I will use my inner drive to excel to help my organization meet its goal.

Practicing Thanks-Giving on Thanksgiving Day

Thursday is Thanksgiving Day. Most of us are aware of our blessings, be they within our families, country or the work place. Within our differing traditions, we express our appreciation in prayerful ways.

This is also the time of year to turn to one another as physicians and employees to express our gratitude. Many of us in direct clinical care and administration often hear words of appreciation, but those who work in supportive roles often do not. We need to change that and go out of our way to thank those who are overlooked. We know who they are.

Here are some suggestions. Express a kind word to those who:

- Carry hammers, pull cable, and open clogged drains.
- Remove scuff marks and polish the floors during night hours.
- Work in labs and draw blood for hours on end.
- Care for Alzheimer patients.
- Stand at the same table in the kitchen day after day, never seeing a patient, yet expertly slicing box-loads of vegetables.
- Counsel the psychiatric and addicted patients.
- Spend days in cubicles focusing on codes and bills.
- Process our pay and cut checks for vendors.
- Volunteer their time and talent giving directions in the lobby.
- Track quality measures in never-seen offices.
- Work as office assistants in hospitals, treatment centers, or in off-campus business offices.
- Upgrade our computers.
- Clean lavatories.

- Staff our physician office practices (even though we only know them by their voices).
- Sweep the grounds and plow the snow.
- Connect thousands of patients by phone to their families.
- Operate the coffee carts.
- Serve as ambulance crews.
- Purchase supplies.

These are the people who make a hospital thrive. Without the contribution of every single person, the hospital would fail to function well. They give us the chance every single day to bring out the best in ourselves.

There is one more group for whom we need to be grateful: patients. If you have contact with patients, try to find ways to express, sensitively and appropriately, your appreciation to those who have entrusted you with their lives. Perhaps a word, glance, touch or kindness is all that is needed.

Today, I will express my appreciation to the people in my life.

Influence

Whenever we elect a new president, or when a new pope is chosen, or when a company changes CEOs, the people who are looking to this person for guidance have the opportunity to think about their expectations. We read about the new person in the paper and wonder what qualities he or she will bring to the post.

It is interesting to consider that all of us are leaders, whether we know it or not, whether we have the title to prove it or not. Everyone in a hospital setting is a leader, not just the physicians and the head administrators. Think about it this way: everybody influences everyone else. Our attitudes and the way we relate to others, shape the work place and impact the feelings and behavior of those around us.

It can be a real stretch to believe that this principle applies to everyone. It is tempting, for instance, to think that the guys who repair faucets or scrub marks off the walls, are merely followers. Yet we can feel their presence throughout the work space as much as the shift supervisor's, charge nurse's or department head's. We may not always be specifically aware of it, but we are influenced by how this person holds himself, by the quality of his presence, and by the attitude he exhibits.

None of us can escape the responsibility of the influence we exert on those around us, whether it is for good or for ill. We can try to get away from it by underestimating it, but it is there nonetheless. Often, we pull back from taking responsibility for the power we have over people and our surroundings because it seems so much easier that way. Yet it is so very important to our lives that we don't do this, because during every moment that we are influencing another person, we are being given an opportunity to learn and to make a contribution. Think of it. What if we went to work every day and conducted ourselves as if we really counted, as if what we did really mattered? How would that change our days?

When Catholics elect their pope, the man changes his name. The Cardinal who was chosen to succeed Pope John Paul, changed his name to Benedict, an act that perhaps reminded him that he now must not only *do* more but *be* more. Whenever someone addresses him, he is reminded of St. Benedict, his namesake, who was a remarkable leader.

If you had the opportunity to change your name into an identity you would like to grow into, what would you change it to? It doesn't have to be from someone famous. I would take my father's name, John. He is long deceased, but I vividly remember his quietness, strength and warmth — qualities I greatly admire. At this time in my life, I feel that I need them more than ever.

Within health care, each one of us needs to have the qualities of a leader if we are to become the best at what we do. We are all needed. What qualities do you bring to the table? Have you accepted the fact that you influence others in the way you work?

Our decision to be the best at what we do, to become more than we are will have a lasting impact on those around us. We need to remember that we are all leaders within our own daily world.

I will always be challenged to live up to my own best self. The decisions I make daily about my attitude and behavior will affect the lives of many people around me.

The Power of Touch

Most patients appreciate the medical care they receive. We can enhance their healing in small but meaningful ways during this stressful time in their lives. Here's a story showing how two nurses made that happen.

A nurse-supervisor was making her rounds when a patient stopped her in the hallway. He told her that he had recently undergone a procedure to contain a serious cancer. The operating room had been cold and sterile and the table was hard. As he lay there, he was afraid and anxious. Then, one of the nurses who was readying him for treatment touched his arm. Another nurse stroked his hair while positioning him on the table. That simple human touch put him at ease, gave him great comfort, and was enormously reassuring. There was something very special about it. Maybe it reminded him of his mother's intimate, tender touch when he was a child. Maybe it was a kind gesture that communicated human warmth and connection, something many of us simply don't experience very often. For whatever reason, the nurses' touch was terribly important.

"I have heard that hospitals are good at treating symptoms," the patient went on, "but not so good at treating people. I don't feel that way here. I felt that I was being treated, not just my cancer, and I wanted you to know how important that was."

It is possible to be technically proficient and have great clinical outcomes and yet fail to heal the patient. These nurses knew this. Do you think hospitals, physician practices, residences and treatment centers could be transformed if we all became aware of our influence on one another and on our patients?

Today, I will be aware of the power I have to touch the lives of others in a deep and meaningful way.

Humility

Yesterday, as I stood behind a surgeon in the cafeteria line, we exchanged small talk. "Doing anything for fun these days?" I asked, expecting him to tell me about wilderness skiing, which I knew he loved. Instead, he was unusually pensive. "No, not really," he said quietly. In our previous talks, he was always funny and quick to engage.

After a minute went by he said, "I just lost a patient. She was elderly, but her heart was strong so we decided it was all right to operate. The procedure was a success, but I just received a call. They told me she stroked." As he paid the cashier, his movements were stilted. This was all he told me. For him, silence was preferable to any further conversation. He seemed far away.

I knew this man well. He is a highly qualified physician, a national leader in his area of expertise. He and his team made an informed clinical decision, took control of the patient's care, and did what their experience told them was correct. Yet the patient died. I knew that this physician's silence was borne of care and a reflection of his sadness, but was he also withdrawn because he now doubted his judgment?

Now and again, all of us are in a similar position. We do what we can. Once we have done our best, we must relinquish control. We have all had the experience of doing our job and expecting a certain result, only to be shocked when the unexpected happens. The experience awakens us to the fact that the world is less controllable than we imagine. This is a humbling experience, especially when we have trained long and hard to be in control. Not one of us is a master of the universe, no matter how good we are at what we do and no matter how hard we try.

Humility, personal as well as professional, is not a value that we talk much about in today's world, yet it remains a remarkably important human value for all of us within the health care community. It joins us in a common understanding that we are limited beings. However, within our limitations we are capable of greatness.

I will use my talents and knowledge to the best of my ability and let go of the results. Humility is compatible with greatness; in fact it allows me to be even better at what I do.

Being the Mayor of Your Own Corner of the World

When we think about individuals who have had a large, positive influence on the world and who seem utterly committed to their work, we may think of some of the heroic figures of our times: Nelson Mandela, Albert Schweitzer and Mother Theresa. And yet, each of us, no matter what our position, will leave a lasting legacy when we love what we do and allow our enthusiasm to touch everyone we meet. We don't have to be in positions where our job is monumental. What we do isn't as important as how we do it.

All of us bring different needs, ideas and motivations to our work. Many of us think of employment primarily as a way to earn the money we need to raise children, maintain a certain lifestyle or just get by. In other words, work is merely a job.

Some individuals, more than we realize, experience work as a vocation. They have an uncommon warmth, humanity and focus that guide them to do ordinary things in the most extraordinary way. They are in cubicles, carrying hammers, cleaning corridors, working in offices and at patients' bedsides.

We can find meaning in our work if we look for it. We may not hold positions where our work or our decisions affect thousands of people. But, we can search for the inner value of our contribution to our work place. Whatever corner of the world we live in—and it might be a lot smaller than the world of a Schwietzer, Mandela, and Mother Theresa— we have a lasting impact on the people in our world.

Think about your day yesterday. Did something unexpected happen that helped you notice how we influence one another? Maybe one of your coworkers offered to cover for you while you made a necessary personal phone call, or your boss made a point of acknowledging a presentation you made in a meeting the other day, or another colleague emailed an article to you about an issue you had been discussing. These are the daily ways we impact one another.

And then, there are the larger ways in which we have a more profound and lasting impact on others. If we have the privilege of working with patients, offering a smile, holding a hand, stroking a forehead, listening to a story through a veil of tears, calming parents, giving children a glass of orange juice, showing kindness—all of these gestures spread good will throughout our corner of the world and in turn we find meaning and satisfaction in our work.

We can look around at the people who share our world. Discovering why our coworkers do the work they do can open our eyes to a different way of thinking about the world and our work. By opening our hearts and minds to new perspectives and understanding about our coworkers, we may touch their lives and also learn more about ourselves. Just having the discussion may be a starting point for finding meaning in our work.

Today, I will think about what makes my work meaningful and how I can influence my corner of the world. I will ask my coworkers why they work and we'll learn and be inspired by one another.

Considering the Patient's Point of View

If we want to provide the best possible clinical care and service, then we have to approach our patients and colleagues with the openness of learners. Too often, we fail to open ourselves up to see that a patient is feeling vulnerable and afraid, and is appealing to us for help. When people are at home, they are relaxed and comfortable largely because it's familiar and predictable. But for most patients, a hospital is an unfamiliar world; one that is foreign and can make them feel uneasy.

The hospital environment has an impact on a patient's state of mind. One of the more telling descriptions of how hospital design influences patients is recounted in the book, *House Thinking*, published by Harper/Collins. The author describes a hospital as an "anti-home" that strips patients of control, privacy, individuality and sleep, while bombarding them with unpleasant sights and sounds. These contribute to illness rather than to healing. If this author is correct, the human element becomes all the more important in giving patients some degree of comfort.

The next time you are with a patient or colleague, look twice. The first glance reveals the usual way we think of them; it is always limited. The second provides an opportunity to see them in a new way.

I will consider the impact of being in a hospital, hospice or medical office from the patient's perspective. As my empathy grows, so does my natural ability to be a healing presence.

$\mathcal{S}$pirituality and Work

Working in health care influences how we live. Every job shapes how we use time, understand the world and even what we believe. Doctors tend to live and think as doctors, nurses as nurses, and carpenters as carpenters. Each develops a particular way of living that fits with the needs of their jobs. This expression of their lives becomes their spirituality. In fact, spirituality is most often described as a way of life.

Many people confuse spirituality with something otherworldly or an activity or system of thought that is confined to churches, synagogues, temples or mosques. Systems of thought that shape how we think of God is theology, not spirituality. Spirituality has to do with the down-to-earth, daily ways that we live our lives. We might use theology to describe how we think about God, and spirituality as the way we live. For a moment, think about spirituality in this way:

- Do our lives allow us time to pull back, read, and reflect?
- Do we get enough sleep?
- Do we have time for family and friends?
- Do we take the kind of vacations that nourish the spirit?

If the answers to these questions are no, we are likely living a spirituality that is unhealthy for us. The state of our spirituality impacts the way we are when we're on the job. It influences every interaction we have. A patient receiving identical treatment from two different nurses will have remarkably different experiences depending on those nurses' spiritual condition. How we do what we do—the kind of presence we bring to work—is of immense significance.

I will think about how I live. If I need to change, I will. Patients need it, my family and friends will welcome it, and I will thrive.

$\mathcal{B}$eing Strong and Vulnerable

Violence has a way of opening a wound in consciousness. On September 11th not so many years ago, we saw the Twin Towers crash to the ground. We were witnesses to thousands of innocent people losing their lives. Watching the tragedy awakened within us the overwhelming and unnerving awareness of our own vulnerability. That could easily have been us and our loved ones. Churches filled, communities gathered, prayers were voiced, tears fell, and strangers embraced. The wound awakened and exposed feelings that the busyness of everyday life usually conceals. We felt vulnerable.

Many of us believe that strength and vulnerability are opposites. The fact is that nobody is stronger than the person who is truly vulnerable because he is making a conscious choice to be open to experiencing a full range of feelings.

We pride ourselves on being strong and self-directed and think of vulnerability as a weakness. Instead of trying to deny our vulnerable feelings, there is value in letting them influence the way we live, both at home and at work.

Remember the way feelings of kinship developed between strangers on the streets of New York, outside Pittsburgh where Flight 93 went down, and Washington where the Pentagon was hit? All around the country, people were opening themselves to their neighbors, to the gas station attendants, to the cashiers at the corner store and to church members. This spontaneous outpouring of openness was an act of pure vulnerability. It awakened empathy.

The expression of empathy generates healing qualities in a hospital setting and in us. To bring a healing presence to those we serve amounts to so much more than being merely technically adept. It is the capacity to be open to the suffering that we see and to use this state of mind to empathize as one human being to another.

I will embrace my feelings of vulnerability and use them to bring a healing presence to my work.

Overcoming Negativity

During a meeting of executives where our desire for organizational excellence was being explained, I overheard an employee saying to the person next to me, "One more unreachable goal being preached by someone out of touch with the way things are."

At first, I was discouraged. His words dampened my excitement. Soon, I was angry. I felt like saying, "Why don't you get on board or find a job that you like?" Luckily, I held my tongue.

I say "luckily" because the man next to me did not need someone speaking angrily to him. That would have made him feel even more frustrated. Everyone genuinely wants to excel. No one wakes up in the morning saying, "I want to be mediocre." Those negative feelings are learned. Buried not so deeply within our hearts are feelings more closely akin to the Marines' motto, "Be the best that you can be."

At the risk of sounding sentimental, naïve, or Pollyannaish, our challenge is to quiet the inner voices that tell us to expect disappointment and mediocrity, and instead listen to the whisperings that lead us to excel.

These are the questions we need to ask ourselves:
- Are you reviewing or developing a bill to be sent to a patient? Make it errorless.
- Are you wiping the brow of someone dying? Do it with care.
- Are you leading a meeting? Do some research, find the best way to lead, and make the time valuable for all.

- Are you a leader? Provide a vision. Awaken, nourish and keep the trust of your employees.
- Are you serving meals? Make sure that the patients receive what they asked for.
- Are you reading a film? Look twice. Your eyes may see what others missed. A patient depends on you.

Today, I will listen to the whisperings that lead me to excel. I will feel better about my work and I will naturally be able to offer more to those I serve.

$\mathcal{H}$ealing with Intention

Recently, I had the opportunity to watch a highly accomplished artist draw a man's face. She would stare at him for a time, then look down at her paper, draw a few lines, and then lift her gaze to study his face again. She must have done this a hundred times, maybe more. She spent much more time looking than drawing. The result was remarkable. Her sketch, while not an exact likeness, caught the personality of the fellow in an astonishing way. She saw what many of us who knew the man, never saw.

How did she do that? She certainly had the training and talent, but there was something else at work. She took time, a lot of time, to notice the person in front of her, and she understood the importance of looking deeply, perhaps even beyond his physical features, to capture his essence.

Do you think patients know the difference between being cared for by someone who is rushed, who simply wants to get the job done, and someone who moves slowly enough and with a conscious awareness of the impact their actions have on the people around them? Do you think our coworkers can sense the same thing?

Reflect on health care as a science and an art. The science part is easy to accept. Understanding the art is more of a challenge. I will acknowledge and nurture the art in what I do by slowing down and working with intention.

Being More Than our Professional Identity

There is an oft-quoted inscription on a tombstone in London that reads, "Here lies Jeremy Brown, born a man and died a grocer." That is a humorous reminder of how easily our lives can become narrowed by work. As the saying suggests, this fellow lost part of himself on his way to becoming a grocer.

We are so much more than the talents we have developed, the roles we play or the titles we carry. In hospitals, with the long work hours, continuous demands and immovable deadlines, it is easy to lose ourselves in relentless activity. We even have name tags to remind everyone how much we are defined by our job title.

Our personal life outside of work may not offer any relief. Often, by the time we go home, we are tired and want to do little more than relax. However, we may have family responsibilities as fathers, mothers, grand-parents, or caretakers for a home-bound family member. It's no wonder our identity can get so tied up in our tasks and responsibilities. Often, we think of ourselves as merely electricians, physicians, office assistants, nurses, lab technicians, or accountants. I once heard a physician say, "I'm always somebody's someone—a mother, physician, sister, aunt, or boss. I wonder if I'm ever myself!" It sounds like she may identify with the grocer, born a woman but died a physician!

We can expand our sense of identity beyond job function by introducing the element of humanity into our daily work experiences. This can be seen in the simplest of tasks—for example, a nursing student who not only makes a patient's bed perfectly, but remembers to call her by name and asks if there is anything else he can do for her. When that nurse dies, no one will say of him that he was born a man but died a nurse. He was born a human being and died a human being. The mark he leaves at this hospital is far more than merely the proficiency he demonstrated in the specialized aspects of this job. It's the way he touches the people around him.

Today, I will be true to myself and to my profession without sacrificing who I am. I will bring who I am into what I do.

Avoiding Burnout

In health care, hardly a day passes that we could call "normal." In our line of work, the people we deal with on a daily basis come to us with all kinds of conditions, some severe and some moderate. Combine that with ever-changing technology, and we have a thoroughly unpredictable situation—every day. For some of us, this unpredictability is part of the challenge and appeal that draws us into the field.

Some say that one reason so many health care professionals become burned out is that they have to numb themselves to the intensity of life about them simply to survive. This shield is a way to avoid feeling the suffering of others. Anyone in a field that deals with human misery—like welfare workers, homicide investigators or firefighters—are confronted by the rawness of life in a way that the rest of the population is not. They, like us, have to make a choice about how much of the suffering of others to let in and how much to keep at bay. They have to keep out enough to avoid a meltdown and yet not so much that they lose their humanity. For self-preservation alone, they have to maintain some sense of balance because they're in this for the long run.

Everyone handles this problem differently. Victor Frankl was a famous physician, psychiatrist and healer who faced the ultimate human nightmare of living through the holocaust. He then graced us with his writing. At one point in his practice as a physician, he noticed two nurses who worked in the same office performing similar procedures but approaching them in completely different ways. One found her job drudgery; the other thought it was the most meaningful work she could ever imagine. The difference was in their awareness. One thought of herself as helping others; the other considered herself merely a machine giving shots.

For those with direct patient contact, it's a matter of knowing how much of the suffering of others we can take in without hurting ourselves. But even if we're not on the front lines of patient care, we can still choose how much of ourselves we want to make vulnerable and open to the human condition. This may come up in our dealings with our coworkers' personal lives, or once-removed as we support our colleagues as they go through trying emotional experiences in the course of their work with patients.

It may seem that if we allow ourselves to be open and transparent to everyday sufferings, we will become depressed. But in fact, we will find that this approach will enrich our lives and give meaning to our work.

This moment, like every moment, provides an invitation to awaken to the sacredness of the ordinary world. Today, I will pause and reflect on the meaning of my work. I will choose to make myself open to the suffering of others.

Going Beyond the Obvious

On a recent flight to Denver, the pilot left the cockpit and personally greeted every passenger while looking them in the eye. His words to my wife and I were, "Welcome, I'm glad you're aboard."

After he finished his rounds, he returned to the cockpit and made an announcement. "Welcome, I'm your captain. We will take every effort to make this trip both pleasant and safe. I have three children. The First Officer also has three. We wouldn't be flying if we didn't feel safe. Now settle back and enjoy the ride." Curiously, I was not aware of being anxious before he came through the cabin. However, I must have been, because afterwards, I felt particularly calm. One man, doing his job, made a difference on that plane. He set a tone, and created a tangible feeling of safety and caring.

There are pilots who are good at the technical side of flying. There are also pilots who know how to be personable leaders as well. Our pilot fell into the second group. He spoke to the more complex needs of the customers not only to arrive in one piece, but to have peace of mind along the way. In other words, he addressed his passenger's unspoken fears of flying.

Patients enter a hospital with many unspoken fears. Most of the time they don't say a word either because they're not in touch with their feelings or they're embarrassed to express them. Some do not want to make waves. For the most part, they have an underlying belief in the technical proficiency of the professional taking care of them, yet most of them secretly yearn to be reassured anyway that they are in good hands and that we care as much about their well being as they do.

We can take our profession to the next level by understanding our patients' needs beyond the unspoken.

Today, I will remember that patients may be unable to voice their fears. I will do what I can to calm their fears and create a feeling of safety.

*L*ove in Action

Walking down the long corridor of the oncology unit late one evening, I paused to look into a patient's room and noticed a nurse sitting quietly on the side of a bed holding the hand of an elderly, closed-eye patient. In another room, a caregiver raised the head of a particularly weak man to help him swallow. In a third room, an aide was changing the soiled linen of a patient's bed.

I wondered how these caregivers do this, hour after hour, day after day. Don't they get discouraged seeing so many helpless patients? How did they develop sensitivity to the needs of their families, particularly those of dying patients? How do they keep their warmth and good humor when faced with so much suffering?

Maybe it is because they think as Paul who said, "...love bears all things, believes all things, hopes all things, endures all things. Love never ends."

There is no way to write love into a job description. No one gets paid extra if they add that component to their work. Only you can recognize how much it contributes to the quality of your work. While we may be hesitant to use this word in a work setting, love still might be the most appropriate word to describe the quality of service from those caregivers as I observed it on the oncology unit that night, and as I have seen it time and again within hospice.

If you are afraid to use the word because it seems too sentimental, just wander through hospital corridors and in and out of patient rooms, watch the staff quietly tending to their patients and it will challenge that way of thinking. There is nothing maudlin about those who care for patients, particularly patients who are helpless and facing death.

Hospice has something else to teach us. We know that its whole job is to help people face their own imminent death and confront all the fear that brings up. Hospice workers know that nothing conquers fear better than love. Death has a way of simplifying life. "[Even if I can] move mountains, but do not love, I am nothing," said St. Paul. Love can be found everywhere: in kitchens, operating rooms, cubicles, patient rooms, nursing stations, and offices of every sort. Sometimes, we simply forget to notice.

We do need our machines, monitors, specialized techniques, and advanced medical procedures. Emails, cell phones, and pagers are equally necessary. However, for a hospital to be called great, it also needs love. We must care for one another—no matter how uncomfortable we may feel using the language that describes it.

Today, I won't be afraid of the word "love" when I think about the work I do. I will see the power of love all around me, as a healing force among colleagues, between caregivers, patients and their families.

Respecting Others' Inner Story

My assistant was looking forward to retiring in two months. While she loved her job, she could hardly wait to begin enjoying her retirement years. In fact, she marked the days. "72, 71, 70 ..." We could all feel her excitement. Amazingly, her attention to detail seemed to sharpen rather than diminish as she thought about life-after-work.

For several months, she had been treated for asthma and had been experiencing a lack of energy, but every time she thought about the future, she seemed to get her energy back. Shortly before her last day of work, she was admitted to the hospital with pneumonia. Soon, she was readmitted. That's when we all found out she had cancer. Treatment began. She never did return to work.

I had known this woman for years. We worked closely together, yet I did not guess the burden she carried. Until the end, neither did she. Sometimes, we are even a mystery to ourselves. With that recognition in mind, it is important to understand that even with the people we work with day in and day out, we will never see every dimension of their lives, the burdens they carry or their loves.

I will recognize the inner life of colleagues that may look different from what I see on the outside. I will acknowledge and respect them for their inner life and for the struggle they are experiencing.

Work as a Sacred Act:
Creating Places of Healing

Let's use today to reflect on the significance of what we are doing. Whether we are mopping a floor or changing a bed, we are actually creating a place of healing. No wonder some philosophers and theologians think of work as participating in the work of God. We are co-creating, and there is a sacredness about our work.

Recognizing the sacredness of what we do—whatever our responsibilities might be—can be unsettling. Why? Because we realize that nothing we do is insignificant; every act shapes this world for better or worse, and we are responsible for whatever we do—or don't do.

Today I will recognize the sacredness of my work. I will be aware that I am creating a place of healing. I will also acknowledge the efforts of a colleague.

Taking Personal Responsibility

Good leaders inspire others. They demonstrate their willingness and ability to take personal responsibility for the very thing they are asking others to do. If a nursing manager has spent years taking care of patients, she can speak with authority and credibility when she asks other nurses to take on a new task.

When Peter Drucker was asked what makes a good leader, he recalled studying about World War I in his high school history class. One of the students asked the teacher why one side won while the other lost when all the factors were basically equal. "After all, during that war, men fought one another in hand to hand combat, often advancing from one fox hole to the next, as they pushed forward or retreated. And, the armies were about the same size."

The teacher quickly responded. "Because not enough generals were killed." This shocked everyone until he explained that the generals on one side lacked leadership. They weren't willing to stand behind their decisions enough to put their lives on the line, so they couldn't generate the necessary commitment from their troops to win.

Effective leaders are always out in front. This is a dangerous place to be, especially if they are in the line of fire. But they are obligated to take the same risks they ask others to take.

Within hospitals, clinics, treatment centers and physician practices, we are not engaged in a battle. However, all of us are leaders because those around us are heavily influenced by our attitudes and actions. Whether or not we have that title, we must be willing to step out, to speak up, and have the courage to take responsibility for our efforts and those of our team.

There are different levels of personal responsibility. It's one thing to take personal responsibility for one's own life. It is another to take personal responsibility within a group, especially if we are not the designated leader. Since we work within groups, it is easy to hide, to relinquish accountability, and to wait for others to take responsibility for what needs to be done. That's a set up for failure for any organization.

Given the risks involved in taking personal responsibility at work, why should we do it? Because when we take personal responsibility, we create a healing environment. Patient care is advanced when every physician, nurse, office assistant, and all support staff recognize that they are leaders.

George Eliot wrote that, "It is never too late to be what you might have been." It is never too late to be a leader. The opportunity is as close as the next encounter with a patient or colleague.

Today, I will consciously take responsibility for my work and for my life. I will test out the title, "leader" and see how it feels and how it changes the way I work and the attitude I bring to my work.

Valuing Everyone's Job

The origins of Labor Day as a holiday rose during a time when laborers had few rights and even fewer days away from their jobs. While the social and political issues that led to the formation of the labor movement in the late 1800s have changed, the opportunity to recognize and celebrate the value of our work has not.

Every one of us contributes to patient care. A nurse's work is invaluable. A physician's irreplaceable. So is the unit clerk's, electrician's, transporter, and the people who work in an office off-site making sure that the patient's files are accurate, that safety is maintained, and that we provide the highest quality of service to those who trust us with their care.

For every person who touches a patient, there are three unseen employees supporting that caregiver. Every one is needed. While we may have differing gifts, no one individual need be valued more than another.

Find a moment to recall the value of what you are doing and the importance of your organization's mission. There is a sacredness in what we do.

Today, I will reflect on the importance of all of the jobs in my work setting. I will think about how all of us are interconnected and how all of our jobs are important in achieving our overall goal of providing high quality patient care.

*R*ising *Above Our Pain*

Yesterday, I marveled at how an employee spoke with a disgruntled visitor to the hospital. While five or six persons were waiting for the elevator, one of them was clearly agitated. He bellowed out to no one in particular, "The valet who parked my car didn't even ask if I needed a wheelchair. I had to walk here." His manner was so forceful that it silenced everyone in the elevator. In that uncomfortable moment, a nurse turned toward him and said in the most disarming way, "I'm sorry. How can I help you now?"

How was she able to do that? What gave her the presence of mind to respond with that kind of empathy? Evidently, she was able to see beyond his gruff manner and pick up on his more vulnerable feelings. The nurse did not seem intimidated by his aggressive manner.

When I went up to visit patients the other day, I was told of a 55-year old woman who was being referred to hospice because of advanced cancer. Amazingly, years ago her child had died of a similar type of cancer at the age of six. She was not belligerent the way the visitor on the elevator was. On the contrary, she was soft-spoken and questioning. "Why is this happening to me? To our family?" She could have allowed her pain to transform into anger and a sense of injustice. Instead, she bore her pain with dignity.

All of us carry painful memories. It may help to know that we can use our pain to develop more empathy to care for others.

As health care professionals, we do not have the luxury to let our personal pain surface and drive us toward a preoccupation with ourselves. We have to be able to distance ourselves from our personal pain long enough to be present to others. The nurse waiting for the elevator seemed able to do this. That is a gift that we all need.

We will have "bad days." However, if these bad days extend into months or years and we cannot get over our preoccupation with our problems, we should not be in health care. Our patients need professionals who can focus on their needs.

We are engaged in a profession where we must place our patients' needs first. It is easy to say this, but difficult to do. No wonder health care is said to be a calling as well as a job.

If I'm going through a difficult time and the pain is still too fresh to allow me to be a healing presence, maybe I should take a short break from my job. Perhaps with time, I can use my painful experience as a source of empathy and healing.

Living an Examined Life

A few years ago, Eugene O'Kelly, age 53, the Chairman and CEO of the huge accounting firm KPMG, was told by his physician that he would probably die of an aggressive brain cancer within three months. He did. But before he died, he decided to write of his experience in a book entitled *Chasing Daylight: How My Forthcoming Death Transformed My Life*. The memoir documents how it did. He said he wrote it for everyone who will die—that is, all of us.

In the book, he explains that he took four actions.

First, he decided against chemotherapy. "It may buy time but not much, maybe a few weeks."

Second, he did all the routine things he needed to do, like getting his finances in order and planning his funeral.

Third, he decided to "unwind" his relationships, find closure with the important people in his life. It entailed having final conversations that others seemed to find more difficult than he.

Last, he tried to fill his final days with perfect moments. "I've always focused planning for the future, now I have to learn the true value of the present."

Cornelia Dean, the accomplished author and often critical reviewer of books wrote, "The meditations on turning ordinary experiences into perfect moments is perhaps the most useful guidance he offers to those of us not yet facing the timetable he confronted. Finding perfection in the

mundane is a skill too many leave underdeveloped, and undervalued."
(*NYTimes*, 3/14/06)

Maybe there is a Eugene O'Kelly in all of us. In this memoir, he does not counsel us to drop from the workforce. Nor does he devalue the need to plan for the future and passionately engage in life. He does challenge us to relish the present, something he had forgotten until he heard the words "about a hundred days" from his doctor.

His wife, child, and colleagues thought of his life as a gift to them. His gift to us is the reminder that each of us has a profound life beneath the frenetic pace with which we sometimes live. We, too, are invited to live an examined life.

I will make the time to be still today. In that stillness, I will examine my life. Is this the life I want to lead? What changes can I make today?

Taking Personal Responsibility for Patient Safety

While we make every effort to ensure the safety of our patients, medical errors happen even at the best of hospitals, and often at a much greater rate than any of us wish to admit. When these errors occur, it is especially heartbreaking and disturbing since we are deeply committed to healing not harming.

When an error occurs, blaming a clinician, caregiver, group or department will not fix the problem. Instead, we—as individuals and as a team—must face the error, identify the elements that led up to it, and collectively take responsibility for it. These are the first steps in creating a culture focused on keeping our hospitals safe.

But how can we promote a culture of patient safety if we don't feel safe about speaking out when we see a problem? We cannot. We must create a culture in which we are free to tell the truth without fear of losing our jobs.

Unfortunately, we sometimes have to reveal problems anonymously. In healthier cultures, we can bring the issue up directly to a manager or to other team members. If our hearts and intentions are squarely on the goal of improving safety we will be heard.

Together, we can create a work place that is committed to safety not just in words but in actions.

Am I doing all that I can to make my work place safe today? Today, I'll have the courage to speak out and work collaboratively to create a safe work place.

Remembering that We Belong to One Another

This evening, many of our patients, staff, and physicians will begin to observe Passover. These are days of remembrance filled with gratitude and hope, notwithstanding the memory of past slavery and oppression. On Thursday, Friday and Sunday, Christians will celebrate the memory of the death and resurrection of Jesus. These days are also filled with the sentiments of forgiveness and the promise of life on the other side of death.

Many of our patients are active within their churches, synagogues, temples, and mosques. During these special days, let's remember again that even though we have differing beliefs and vastly differing views of the world, we share a common humanity where our differences can be seen as truly a gift.

As Mother Teresa reminded us, "If we have no peace, it is because we have forgotten that we belong to each other." Despite all our differences, we must strengthen the belief that we belong to one another. It is easy to forget this sentiment in the rush of a day filled with responsibilities.

This week, holy week on many calendars, is another timely reminder of the countless opportunities we have to care for others at home, in love relationships, with strangers and at work.

Today, I will look for ways to connect with my coworkers, patients, their families and my loved ones by reflecting on what it means to "belong to one another."

Continuous Learning

During the monthly meeting of physician executives, it was reported that our nursing partnership with one of the community colleges had been highly successful. "We have thirty students, most with their bachelor degrees, all engaged in a one year accelerated nursing program." Then she added, "One of the students is a practicing physician." Here we had a doctor at the pinnacle of his career who found it necessary to go back to school because he wanted to enhance his knowledge.

We seldom hear of a physician enrolling in a nursing program. By taking the unusual step of returning to school, that physician suggested that he was aware of the need to continuously learn. The longer we practice our profession, the easier it is to overlook this need.

While we may not be inclined to return to formal schooling, all of us need to be learners especially in medicine because technology changes so rapidly. When we recognize the need to learn, our gratitude and appreciation for one another grow as we realize that everyone has something to share with us.

We all learn from one another. Colleagues are our teachers and so are patients. Turn toward them with an attitude of learning and patient care will be enhanced. Even our children are affirmed when we learn from them. And, to the physician who has enrolled in nursing school, thank you.

Whether through formal schooling or through the daily opportunities that arise at work, I will see my colleagues, patients and all with whom I come in contact as my teachers.

Being Honest

When we read about athletes or business magnates, or listen to stories about people in the news, it is striking how our attention is turned to the value of honesty. In so many stories, we can see that self-interest, greed and the need for immediate gratification squeeze out integrity. For some, there's more of a pull to meet their own needs than to do the right thing.

We see how dishonest individuals can be when judging skating performances that favor their own country, how athletes use drugs to give themselves an unfair advantage, and how executives of major corporations tolerate and sometimes sanction an executive culture of deceit. All of these news items test our trust in organizations and people.

The attempt to be honest is a shared human struggle. As employees within health care organizations, we have to continually ask ourselves if we are being ethical as well as powerful. Do we take enough trouble to protect the individual? Do we bill accurately? Do we document truthfully? Are managers free of conflict of interest when they select vendors? Do doctors favor one drug company over another? Do we speak the truth even if it might put our jobs on the line? These are daunting questions. How we answer them says a great deal about how much integrity we have.

Usually, we think of honesty in terms of behavior, that is, whether what we do is right or wrong. But, we can also think of it in terms of being honest with ourselves.

We are all valuable, but no one is worth more than any other. When we slip into thinking of ourselves as better, more important, or more valued than others, it won't be long before we act as if we're entitled. Just as unfortunate, we can learn to think of ourselves as less valuable than others. That is equally destructive. It is also dishonest because it is not true.

When we are honest with ourselves and with one another, we can't help but become in touch with the universality of the human condition, which levels the playing field, and opens us up to deeply appreciating and valuing our colleagues' unique talents. It releases the tremendous energy of love and tolerance in our dealings with others. It all begins with you and me.

I will be honest with myself and with others. By being true to myself and to others, I grow as a person. Honesty is an eternal value.

Attitude Adjustment at Work

Three news items relate to how our attitude influences who we are at work, how we do our job, and how we influence others and the work place in general. The first article found in a professional publication covers depressed individuals who tend to be more absent-minded on the job, and it reveals how this emotional state seriously affects their performance. The second article from a local newspaper reports on unionization efforts taking place at two hospitals. The nurses who were interviewed expressed frustration and outrage over what they viewed as unreasonable demands from administrators to interact more with patients and families. The third article comes from a national newspaper. It reported on the retirement of a nun who had cared for neglected children selflessly and without acclaim. Each of these articles illustrates the impact that our attitudes have on the quality of our work, and conversely, on the impact that work has on us and our quality of life.

First: The Journal of the American Medical Association's (JAMA) special report on the topic of depression. The research studies noted the prevalence of depression within the general population and how it remains an under-treated disease. One of the authors coined the word "presenteeism" ("here but not here," a play on the word "absenteeism") to describe those who show up, but who work absent mindedly precisely because they are depressed. Several authors suggested that these individuals brought their problems to work rather than found them there. When people are struggling with their own unhappiness, it's hard for them to be generous with others.

Second: The article in a local newspaper reporting on the efforts to unionize two local hospitals. The reporter quoted several nurses who spoke of poor working conditions, low morale, and administrators who laid "burdensome" rules on them—including the request that they put people first and the suggestion that they be pleasant when serving patients!

Third: Sounding a different note, the New York Times's article on the retirement of a 75-year-old sister. She left her job as the administrator of Covenant House—the worldwide organization of homes serving teenage street people. It was a touching account of a dedicated woman who devoted her life to care for unwanted children. This is an unnoticed woman who, throughout her life, clearly brought an attitude of sympathy, selflessness and unconditional love into her work.

What do these three seemingly disparate articles have in common? They identify how our attitudes help shape the work place. The JAMA article points out the prevalence of depression. The local unionization article highlights how attitudes of resentment, borne of depression and perhaps burnout, make even the most basic of job requirements—courtesy and compassion—burdensome, and how this collective negativity is like a poison. From a different angle, the New York Times article shows how a sister with a selfless, loving attitude and no need for recognition, shapes the culture of her work place.

These articles highlight in very different ways how the attitudes that we bring to our work cannot be separated from the quality of the work that we do. So, if we can become aware of our disposition (depressed, resentful or generally happy), we can see how this affects our work. And through awareness, we can take steps to adjust our attitude, not only so that we can feel better about our work, but also about ourselves and our lives.

Take a fresh look at your coworkers and notice the number of high-functioning, caring, dedicated individuals with whom you work. We learn from one another, and what is truly surprising is how we are changed when we express our appreciation of who they are and how they work.

Today, I will reflect on the attitude I bring to my work. I will look at my coworkers with new eyes and find ways to express my appreciation for who they are and what they do.

*T*he Quiet Reality
Underneath the Busyness

This has been an incredibly busy week. Next week, it will probably be the same because sickness and death will always be with us. No one will say to us, "Don't worry, you don't have to take care of me today. Just come back when you're relaxed." Seven days a week, twenty-four hours a day, blood needs to be taken, lab tests run, rooms readied, and meals provided.

We don't cease to be human when we choose to become health care professionals, yet our work demands that we operate at a machine-like rate, a machine with parts that never wear down.

However, when we remember the quiet reality that is underneath all the busyness, work can be a prayer. It is a wordless kind of prayer that is expressed through caring hands, thoughtful gestures and loving heart.

Wherever we work, whatever we do, and however busy we are, we can remember that work is hallowed action. This is an invaluable perspective that changes how we think about work.

I will take time despite my busyness to slow down and know that there is another reality being served in all that I do. My hands, my efforts and my intentions all contribute to a healing and a deeper reality. My work and my life take on a deeper meaning and everyone is better served.

*S*lowing Down and Feeling Connected

This morning I awoke around 2 a.m.; I turned on the radio and Aaron Copeland's Letter From Home was playing. Words cannot describe the feeling of listening to that piece in the silence. My wife was sleeping, the lights of the city were bright, but there were no cars or people to be seen. The combination of darkness, lights, my wife sleeping, stillness and the music were striking. The music expressed what words cannot: the feeling of being apart, wanting comfort, yet feeling connected.

With the press of everyday activities, we can forget how connected we really are. Unfortunately, it often takes a crisis to awaken to our ever present, deep yearning to connect with one another.

One of our employees was called for military service. After he returned, he said, "I really appreciated all the people in my department who wrote to me so often. I can't tell you what that meant to me. Unless you were there, you can't understand."

Those of us who are home may not fully comprehend, but we can make a conscious decision to make gestures that connect us with others. A phone call or a note can keep us in contact with those who are apart.

Today, I will slow down and feel the deep connection that I have with family, friends, coworkers and patients. I will express the appreciation I have for them.

$\mathcal{E}$xpressing Gratitude Without Words

The experience of loss is often the soil from which gratitude rises. My father died when I was a teenager. As the years pass, the memories of him become even more vivid. Yet, I also live with the regret that I didn't get to know him as an adult. I suspect, however, that if he were living, I would take his presence for granted and not realize that every day I had with him was a gift.

Soon after the September 11th attack, I was listening to a reporter interviewing a cameraman who was severely injured in the collapse of the Twin Towers. He had the good fortune to have been rescued by firemen. When asked on television if he wanted to thank those who rescued him, he began to cry. "Words of thanks do not come close to expressing what I feel." He continued to cry and did not utter a word of thanks. He did not have to. The very depth of his emotions communicated how he felt. Interestingly, the firemen didn't have to speak either. They, too, let their feelings speak for themselves.

Words are important, but how we are present to one another is even more so.

Today, I will try to express my gratitude through words and also through my way of being.

Embracing a Fresh Perspective

For those who have been in health care for years, we have to keep perspective on our work. Here are examples of two people in vastly different careers, who used their own experiences to broaden their perspective.

A highly decorated pilot and astronaut returned to earth after being in orbit six months with two Russian cosmonauts. Earlier in his career as a fighter pilot, he had flown missions against the Russians. Reporters asked him how he was able to work so closely with people who had once been his enemy. He replied, "When I see and hear of people in conflict, I remember what it was like to look at earth from afar. From that distance, it is obvious that earth is small and its people dependent one on the other. I thought how petty, petty, petty. I wish everyone could travel in orbit. We are a lot smaller than we think." It is remarkable how dramatically one person's perspective can shift.

In a second example, a nurse shared her experience of working over the winter holidays. "This year, I had to be on duty the week between Christmas and New Year's. Work just seemed different. The census was down, there were fewer cars in the parking lot, and other nurses were taking time off to be with their families. I started feeling sorry for myself until I thought about the soldiers in Iraq and how far away from home they must feel. My thoughts also turned to the homeless, to prisoners, and to the aged living alone. None of these people were having the 'traditional' family Christmas with trees and lights and a turkey with stuffing. And then, there were the hospice patients right on my floor. What was their experience of 'the holidays'? Having this perspective lead me straight out of my self-pity."

Everyone in health care knows that it is easy to become run down. Finding a fresh perspective invigorates us and our careers!

Today, I will not be afraid to take time out of my day for reflection. I will embrace the new perspective that emerges.

$\mathcal{L}$eading with Courage and Faith

David McCullough's book, *1776*, could just as well have been titled, "George Washington" because most of its text describes his leadership style. Without significant support from the government that appointed him, without money, without a professional army, Washington inspired his troops, and eventually won a war that seemed, at times, unwinnable.

All those who signed the Declaration of Independence also needed personal courage. At the time of the signing, victory was far from assured. Many signees lost their property and their lives as a result of signing. George Washington, while an effective leader, suffered lingering bouts of depression. Numerous times, he offered his resignation to Congress. He not only doubted himself, but others criticized him for his indecisiveness.

We, too, need courage. We will likely not be killed, lose our homes or be jailed because of our beliefs. Yet, there is a cost involved when we accept our role as leaders. If our efforts don't pay off, our reputation may be tarnished, we may suffer a disappointing outcome, and relationships may become strained.

History has been kind to General Washington and to the founding fathers. Historians agree that he was a remarkable leader and whatever doubts they had, they did not let them get in their way. In spite of our own doubts about our ability to lead, we cannot stand back and be passive. Is the effort worth it? Yes.

I will take responsibility and bring understanding and courage into all that I do. I will be willing to make the necessary sacrifices if it means greater healing for others. I will also be rewarded with a feeling that I've done my best and brought the best of myself to my work.

Recognizing the Invisible Heroes

At a celebration honoring our faithful employees, the administration treated everyone to a film at the local IMAX theatre. As they were leaving the theater, an employee standing in line remarked to her guest, "The nice thing about movies is that when they're over, the names of the people who contributed to the film are listed. When you work in health care, there are no acknowledgements at the end of the day!"

For every employee who works directly with patients, there are three who work behind the scenes to support them. These key people are often invisible. We take their work for granted. An evening honoring long-service employees is one reminder of how many individuals work self-lessly, year after year, behind the scenes, in jobs that are immensely important though not often recognized. There are never enough awards to acknowledge those deserving recognition.

Consider those in buying, billing, or sterile processing. Is their work and presence affirmed often? Think about those in Central Supply working the night shift to replenish supplies to be used the next day, the employees who work continuously to organize patient records, the EAP counselors who respond to employees-in-need, or to the hundreds of unnamed employees who work behind the scenes to maintain our hospitals, treatment centers, and offices.

There is goodness, engagement, and dedication all around us! Seeing goodness changes how we think, what we say, and how we do what we do. When you pass someone in the hallway, take a moment to say, "Nice job." Send an email to tell a coworker how much her idea made your job easier. When you work as a team, before everyone disperses, offer a word of appreciation. Our challenge is to find ways to express our appreciation continuously. The opportunity is as close as the next moment.

Today, I will start the trend of thanking my coworkers for their good work. I can change my work environment with this small but important act.

Making a Mark

After a chaplain returned from being with hospice patients one day, she said to me quietly, "This work really makes a mark on me."

The Chief Executive Officer of a hospital who was returning to work following hip replacement surgery, started an early morning meeting by commenting, "I'm not a real demonstrative person when it comes to prayer, but I'll tell you that being a patient has really left a mark on me. When you are going under anesthesia, you can't help thinking about things a little differently. I'm grateful I can return to work and I'm grateful for our staff. I pray for the courage and strength to do what has to be done to improve patient care."

The phrase "making a mark" has been used throughout history. It is used in the Hebrew Scriptures to describe Jacob's wrestling with an angel; the struggle left a permanent mark on his thigh. The chaplain, the CEO and Jacob all went through life-altering experiences and their perspectives were forever changed.

The experiences of illness and injury also shape the way we see things. Patients are transformed by illness. When someone is hospitalized, bedridden or in pain, life slows down and he sees the world differently. The experience rearranges his priorities. Afterwards, he lives and works in a different way.

What is true for patients is also true for health care professionals. No one can be in health care for long without being "marked." Many of us labor in offices, kitchens or workshops. Whether or not our work brings us in direct contact with patients, we have an opportunity—even a responsibility—to bring a healing presence to others. To do this, we must let illness make its mark on us. It is a remarkably good teacher.

I will allow my work to leave its mark on me and use this altered perspective to make me more available to the healing needs of others.

Stop and Breathe to Gain Perspective

Hospitals, like so many businesses, have coffee carts at their entrances. Patients and staff can purchase drinks, sandwiches and snacks. These carts create a welcoming presence as well as provide a needed service.

Something out of the ordinary occurred at one of them last week. Late in the afternoon, twenty or so minutes after closing, the clerk behind the counter was counting money. A young mother, who had just spent the last several hours tending to her own mother in the emergency room, came up to the cart with her small boy, and asked for a bagel to give her son, who had missed lunch. The clerk, who was tired and stressed, said curtly, "The cart is closed." The mother, who was equally anxious, was suddenly beside herself. She needed to placate her cranky child at a time when she was fast approaching a breaking point. An argument ensued and quickly escalated to the point of name-calling as others looked on nervously.

After the woman and vendor left the scene, many of the witnesses were still in the area. One of them noticed my employee badge. She came over to discuss what happened. "Classic. Ugly." she said, "Two stressed out people who couldn't communicate. It's that simple. If the girl behind the counter hadn't been tired, she would have reached for a couple of the unsold bagels, given them to the woman and said 'Here, they're on the house.' If the mother hadn't been panicked about her own mother, she would have just gone to the vending machine down the hall."

Everyone can either add to or dispel tension when tempers are about to flare in a hospital. Sometimes that requires making adjustments and extending ourselves beyond "the rules" because we see the anxiety and desperation just below the surface. In this case, the vendor had not responded with any awareness beyond her own exhaustion and snapped at the mother. If this vendor had recognized the pain beneath the mother's demands, she would have reacted with compassion and given her what she needed. It simply requires transcending the intensity of the moment. The woman who approached me afterwards and sized up the situation, immediately identified a solution. She was only able to do that because she had the comfortable distance of an outsider. This is the value of a detached presence.

When I'm tired or unhappy, I will stop, take a deep breath and collect myself. I will transcend the immediate tension of the moment by remembering the stress that others may be feeling and act from a higher place of compassion.

Gratitude Is a Gift

Within health care, there is a tangible "culture of giving." Large numbers of our colleagues offer their services in numerous ways within their own communities when they are away from work.

But some look to the world at large. I recently received an email from an employee who volunteered her services in Botswana, Africa. This is what she wrote about her experience:

"I've had many insights during the past two weeks. One is how lucky we are back home to have water and electricity. Many times here I have been in places without water or electricity, or both. Now I realize how lucky I am. I hope never to take them for granted again."

In the land of plenty, it's so easy to take things for granted that others consider treasures. A grateful heart is a gift that will change our perception. Once awakened, it will influence what we notice, how we feel, and even how we work. The incalculable reward of being generous comes from the awakening of gratitude within our own hearts.

Gratitude is the unintended gift I receive from giving to others. I will give that gift to myself.

$\mathcal{U}$sing Depression as a Motivation

This was a banner week: JCAHO awarded our hospital full accreditation for the next three years. What made this award even sweeter was that it was unexpected. All week, the surveyors were sending signals that we were failing to meet Standards. We had been working under the expectation of receiving "conditional" accreditation.

When we received notification that we were awarded full accreditation, you could feel a lift in spirits spread from employee to employee. We knew we still needed to improve, but there was also a surge of energy to improve. Soon after the word was out, I was walking past the office of an administrator who had played a significant role in the accreditation process and heard her remark, "I feel so much lighter now."

While she surely wouldn't want to admit to it, I would say that before receiving the news, she and the others had been experiencing a feeling of depression—that is, they were de-pressed, or pressed down. No one likes to be labeled "depressed," so they had been carrying a weight, acknowledged or not. When the administrator said she felt lighter, she revealed how depressed she had been.

The team went through the type of heaviness that comes when individuals who are deeply invested and engaged in a project are disappointed. Anyone who has ever played on a sports team knows what this feels like. The challenge is knowing how to rise above it.

Everyone wants to excel. Is reaching for success risky? You bet. Could you be setting yourselves up for disappointment? Possibly. Is it worth the risk? Yes.

Winston Churchill knew something about achieving remarkable results in the face of defeat. Most people don't know this, but Churchill had experienced nothing but failure throughout much of his life. He lost many elections, he lost the esteem of his family and his colleagues during different periods in his life, and he had spent some years wandering aimlessly, looking for direction. He was a man who knew failure intimately. And yet, toward the end of his life, in an event that forever shaped the course of our world, he rose to his greatest potential during the battle against Adolph Hitler in World War II. As the people of London were being barraged by daily bombings, they clung to his speeches that inspired them to keep up their courage. At a time when England was about to lose a war, his was the voice that they welcomed. He led the country through this ominous period. He understood failure not as an end but as a teacher.

Depression is not a popular topic in the work place. Perhaps one of the reasons we do not want to acknowledge it is because it seems so negative and destructive. What Winston Churchill knew, and we must learn, is the role of courage in our lives. He thought of it as "the ability to go from failure to failure without losing enthusiasm." This is a lesson we must learn, too.

Ups and downs are part of everyday life, especially when one is passionately engaged. To pretend that depression doesn't exist is foolish. A work place where we cannot take time to reflect on life during difficult times would not be a healthy environment. Neither would it be a place of healing.

If I am depressed about the possibility of failing, I will acknowledge that now, take courage, and charge ahead.

Making Your Job Influential and Meaningful

One of the hospital's telephone operators who has worked the lines for more than ten years, remarked how much she enjoyed her work. "People think it's dull, but it's not. My voice creates the first impression people have of the hospital. I like being that person. Besides, if I don't come to work, this place would almost shut down. Families couldn't speak with patients, doctors would miss calls, and frantic people couldn't reach the ED." Even though there was a phone line between her and the callers, she still felt a connection to each person.

She was insightful enough to recognize that while her role in the callers' lives is fleeting, she has an influence. Martin Buber, the great Jewish teacher, said that his hand used to tremble when opening the door of his classroom. He was acutely aware that he could forever shape the minds of those who listened. He was awed by the enormity of the responsibility.

The telephone operator's job might seem to be far down the ladder of importance when we think of our primary function of healing and caring for patients, but she found a way to recognize the significance of her work. This awareness has given her a greater sense of meaning and fulfillment in her work and made her a valuable and decidedly influential presence.

I will see how everyone plays an important and unique role at work, and in the ultimate healing that is taking place. I will see everyone's job—and my own—with fresh eyes, and appreciate the difference we are making in people's lives.

$\mathcal{B}$eing a Force for Healing
When There Is No Cure

Something unusual happened yesterday in the chapel. A patient, knowing that he would die shortly, wanted to marry his fiancée. So he and his bride had their wedding in the hospital chapel. A priest witnessed the ceremony and many from the patient's care team attended. While we celebrated the happy marriage, we prayed, both openly and silently, for his cure. Everyone, none more than the physicians, hoped for it.

Yet last week, he died. The sadness of staff and friends was tangible. One said, "We prayed so hard. He looked so good. It's so discouraging." His wife brought photos of the wedding, which captured his smile and sense of well-being. She and the staff remembered clearly how happy he was on his wedding day.

Those present spoke of feeling his peacefulness. This man may not have been cured, but he was healed. His wife attests to that. While our staff could not cure his disease, he was indeed healed.

Our challenge every day is to be present in a way that heals. When we are, ordinary conflicts and frustrations seem remarkably less important. Sometimes we place too much attention on the technical side of medicine and not enough on the human caring side. Each of us can enhance our human caring side by bringing in an added dimension of selflessness and generosity.

One story that comes to mind is of a woman who requested to be a foster parent to children whom she knew had terminal illnesses. When she was asked how she managed to take care of them without becoming depressed, she said, "The way I look at it is that every life, whether it is long or short, is a complete life. Each person is special. If someone lives to be seventy, that's his life. If he lives to be seven, that's his life. I'm not concerned that I'll become depressed. I'm just trying to do what I can do."

Today, I will look for ways to be more selfless and generous in my interactions with others.

Keeping Perspective About Why We're Here

My wife and I were fortunate enough to take a long-anticipated vacation trip to Italy. Shortly before boarding the plane, the gate attendant announced that it was to be grounded because of weather conditions in Chicago. Those going to Rome would have to be rerouted through London, causing us to arrive four hours later than planned.

The man sitting across from me turned ballistic and even offensive. His wife was so embarrassed that she hit him in the ribs with her elbow. The force would have knocked a lighter man right off his chair. "Be quiet," she said. "If this was your father traveling to Europe by ship, it would have taken him two weeks. If your great-grandfather were making this trip, he would have sailed for months. You've lost your perspective and it's going to ruin your trip and mine!"

Amazingly, the man quieted down. His wife was in the same predicament as he was, yet she was able to quickly step back and view the situation from a broader perspective.

What happened to him can happen to any of us. It is easy to lose perspective when faced with a setback, especially within hospitals, medical offices, and treatment centers where expectations are high, tasks are demanding, and time is short. Disappointment and frustration can quickly take control. There is a high price that comes with a lost perspective. Patients are not served well, we short-change our colleagues, and performance suffers.

Patients think of hospitals as places to go when they're sick. Others see them as employment opportunities, and some as businesses. But none of us can afford to lose sight of the bigger picture—that hospitals are places where people care about others in highly specialized ways. Under stress, the tiniest event may seem like it's the end of the world. The challenge is to find ways to remember that caring is what we are all about.

Today, I will remember why I chose my line of work and strive to keep things in perspective. My work will thrive when I do.

Having an "Attitude"
About Patient Safety

Usually, if someone says you've got an "attitude" about something, it's not a good thing. But when it comes to keeping patients safe while they're in our care, having an attitude about it and a commitment to reducing medical errors is necessary.

Most of the time, we think of safety in terms of needle sticks, falls, or mistaken medication or dosages. We have to eliminate these errors. The National Patient Safety Goals include: Improve the accuracy of patient identification; improve the effectiveness of communication; improve the safety of prescribing medications; reduce the risk of health care-associated infections; accurately and completely reconcile medications across the continuum of care; reduce the risk of patient falls; reduce the risk of influenza and pneumococcal disease in institutionalized older adults.

It's easy to end the discussion of safety with this list. While these actionable points are critical to patient safety, the discussion is incomplete and impossible to fully achieve without talking about something underlying these acts that is even more difficult to achieve and measure: an attitude of safety. What does this mean?

One way to look at safety-as-an-attitude is to think of a mother and her child—especially those fate-tempting toddlers. A mother is always on the alert with her child, carefully watching and anticipating all the injuries that can befall him as he explores the playground, the street or the neighborhood creek. Even during the night, a mother is attentive to her child's sounds. If she places him in the care of a babysitter or preschool, she expects these caregivers to be equally responsible and vigilant. Care drives her vigilance.

When patients come into our facilities, they, too, are expecting us to take care of them with the same level of trust, vigilance and attentiveness. Understandably, our first thought when it comes to patient safety has to do with the immediate, physical actions we can take. And, if we see areas where a patient's care is in jeopardy, we must take the initiative and work within our group to develop detailed policies, processes, and procedures. But patient safety doesn't end there. It begins with attitude. Having an attitude of vigilance, we see things through a "safety" filter and become aware of unsafe procedures that we might otherwise have missed.

Each of us is challenged to develop a culture of safety, not unlike a mother's. You may ask, "Aren't you just adding one more thing on my too-long list of things to do?"

If you were to ask that question of an overworked, overtired mother, what do you think she would say? Probably, "Sorry, I don't even want to go there. It's worth it to me to be safe regardless of the added effort it takes." And so it is with us. It is impractical not to approach all that we do with an attitude of patient safety. This is at the heart of all that we do, of all that we are about.

Today, I will be aware that the care and vigilance I have about my work will contribute to a culture of safety in the work place. When I have the same vigilance over my work as a mother has over her child, safety will naturally follow.

Work and Intimacy

On Valentine's Day, we think of hearts. When hearts are mentioned, health care professionals are likely to think of clinical outcomes or of a service line rather than chocolates or flowers. Of course, when we return to our children, spouses and loved ones, the sentiments associated with the heart take on different meanings.

Beneath the popularization of this holiday lies a deeply embedded yearning within all of us to find others with whom we can share intimacy—the human need to connect with others in a deep way. We can look back on our most intimate moments as times when we understood someone and his or her world deeply, and that person understood ours, in return. We can think of intimacy as a meeting of hearts and minds. Anne Morrow Lindberg writes of it as, "two solitudes touching." It is an overlapping of two beings that has nothing to do with physical contact.

Usually, we think of finding that closeness only with family and friends. Yet, there is intimacy in the work place, too. Our professional training cautions us to honor physical boundaries and adhere to strict codes of conduct prohibiting behavior that may be intrusive and unwelcome. Nevertheless, care givers have many opportunities to experience the deep satisfaction that comes with intimacy.

When we're at work, we do not kiss each other, send flowers, or ask to be someone else's Valentine. Yet, there are intimacies. Think of the shared and often unspoken sentiments that arise when a nurse's aide gives an elderly woman a sponge bath. Watch an OB/GYN deliver a baby, or an anesthesiologist gently reassure a frightened patient before surgery, or a child life specialist organize the pediatric staff to sing Happy Birthday to a 5-year-old boy with leukemia. These moments are intimate as well as gifts.

Valentine's Day is an opportunity to recognize anew the lingering dreams and desires that led us to work as we do. We yearn to be close to others.

I will connect with others by looking for ways to be of service. I will not be afraid to experience intimacy through the service I provide.

The Impact of One

Every hospital is blessed with gifted employees. In many medical centers, as a result of efforts to acknowledge and reward employees, turnover has dropped significantly. Recently, one of our most highly respected employees left the organization. Some knew her only by her title, the Vice President and Chief Operating Officer. The majority of employees and physicians remember Colleen as an experienced, warm, gentle, humorous, and caring nurse. While having administrative responsibilities, she was always a "nurses' nurse." A number of us, even those who did not know her well, thought of her as a friend. She had a way of awakening a feeling of closeness in so many of us. With her leaving, we realized the impact she had on all of us and on our organization.

While our jobs are difficult, why do so few leave? There are probably many reasons. Job satisfaction is one. Another is the fact that almost everyone enjoys being part of a highly motivated team that is doing important work. Striving to provide the best clinical care and seeing a documented increased satisfaction among patients certainly heightens our satisfaction as physicians and employees. Perhaps another is the fact that most employees appreciate their managers and colleagues. When we feel respected, supported, and challenged, it is easy to come to work.

When individuals leave health care, they do so for many reasons. Sometimes it is to get married; at other times, to study or stay at home with their young children. Others are attracted to a new job opportunity. Disconcertingly, some leave because they are dissatisfied with some aspect of their job.

Colleen serves as an example of the impact we can have to inspire, lead and awaken those around us. When our passions support our work lives, our impact will be great and lasting.

What kind of example of my profession am I? I will think about how I can have a positive, lasting impact on those around me and express my appreciation for those who awaken my passion for my work.

Honoring the Call to Be the Best

One of the singers on the public television show, "The Irish Tenors" is a physician. He struggled to decide whether to follow his desire to be a practicing physician or to follow an equally strong, yet subtler pull, to be a musician. When he thought of himself as a physician, he envisioned being "average," "successful," "esteemed," and "of help to others." When imagining himself as a professional musician, he thought of himself as "selfish" (because he enjoyed singing so much!), yet he was more "talented" in this field. He chose music. Perhaps, the music chose him.

Many of us struggle with being pulled in seemingly different directions. The way we resolve (or avoid resolving) that pull has consequences. There will always be a cost, whichever direction we decide to go, and often it is high.

The problem is that most of us, in fear, pull back from moving in the direction we are called. This may feel comfortable, but the cost is mediocrity. Just like the experience of a musician misplaced as a physician.

What is true of individuals may be true for organizations. As we work to create the organization we envision, let us also help one another live reflectively in a seemingly mundane world with its hidden sacredness.

Today, I will choose to excel in all that I do. I will encourage my work place not to settle, but to strive for its vision to excel in all that it does. I will push through my fear and experience the joy of being the best I can be.

Work Differently, Not More

We need to change our approach to work if we want our organization to stay mission-focused. In health care, that means helping it become one that delivers the best possible clinical care and service to patients. That is the single most important tenet of any medical facility. Day in and day out this vision should influence how we use time, what we do, and what we do not do. This is a terribly important issue for a mission-driven organization intent on constantly improving patient care.

Few of us can work harder than we already do, and even if we try to work harder, it may not be healthy or sustainable. Imagine an airplane flying at the highest speed for which it is designed. If the pilot pushes it still further, the plane will rip apart under the strain. People are not much different. Pushing one another to do more only increases our stress, which leads to a loss of heart. Will that improve patient care? Not likely. The challenge is to increase our capacity for achievement. Rather than doing this by physically working harder, we need to review our organization's vision, understand how we can contribute to its achievement, and direct all of our actions toward its accomplishment. We should question any actions or work we do that does not support our organization's vision.

Many of our organizations provide good quality clinical care. So how do we take what we do to the next level? It starts with a highly competent, talented, skilled staff, people who also infuse their work with heart, soul and passion to achieve the organization's mission. Next, it has to be a vision that is shared by everyone in the organization. By stating what this vision is, taking personal responsibility for doing our part to fulfill it, and engaging our hearts and souls in that effort, we lift our organization to the next level (and gain a personal satisfaction with the accomplishment).

Let's look at the power of holding a vision in our heart and mind to achieve an end. Consider the story of Nelson Mandela. One of the things that distinguished him from his fellow prisoners was his steadfast vision. Nelson never wavered in his devotion to democracy, equality and learning. When he left prison after nearly thirty years, he is reported to have said that his years in detention with little to do helped him avoid frenzied activity after he was released. (Imagine trying to "catch up" after being imprisoned for three decades. Where do you begin?)

How did Nelson Mandela organize and prioritize his actions after his release? By embedding in his mind and heart the vision of his countrymen being freed, by prioritizing and selecting only those actions that lead to the fulfillment of that vision. This foundation—the vision of what could be—ordered everything. What did not fit the vision was simply dropped. He didn't work harder, he worked differently.

Think about the health care professionals in other parts of the world who are working under extraordinary conditions—dirt floor huts, no electricity, minimally sanitary conditions, limited equipment and resources to do the job and functioning with very little sleep or personal comforts for weeks on end. All they have sometimes is the power of their own vision to help—no matter how little they have to work with. They are hungry and sleep-deprived and often work 12-hour shifts. A father might walk into the camp one day, exhausted after journeying hundreds of miles over rugged mountain trails. His sick boy is on the back of a donkey. These professionals can't turn the child away because they themselves are tired, cold, burned out or lack resources. How do they bolster themselves to treat this little boy? They must dig down deep within themselves, tap into the passion that brought them into health care in the first place, and go about the business of tending to their tiny patient. Just like them, you can do things you never thought you could do just because you have vision and calling.

Practically speaking, given your situation and responsibilities, review your organization's vision and your role in helping to achieve it. Think about what you have to do to increase your capacity for achievement without falling into the trap of simply trying to work harder.

Today I will be mindful of my vision and my organization's vision and I will tap into the passion that has brought me to this place. I will assess every activity that supports this vision and do it with heart.

The Power of Connecting with Colleagues

Before the physicians' meeting this morning, uncharacteristically, they paused for a few minutes of silence. The silence was followed by one of the doctors mentioning that two hours before the meeting began, he was in the mountains on his bike. It was his birthday. When looking out over the horizon he was mindful that he was now the same age his father was when he died. He paused while speaking and then added, "I like being on a medical staff where we take time to think, I don't mean about practice, but about ourselves. There's a warmth here that I appreciate." When he reflected on his own mortality, he saw the immense value of being able to trust his colleagues enough to reveal an intimate, personal aspect of himself.

His words influenced the whole tone of the meeting. He awakened a sense of commonality, as all of us could connect with what he was feeling once he took the risk of revealing himself. It improved the quality of our whole day.

We are always in need of connecting with our coworkers. One way is to take time now and again to reveal something about ourselves at work. We may resist this because we don't think we have time for such intimate discussion; we may think it is inappropriate to reveal more of ourself in a work setting. Some feel that it interferes with their ability to get things done; others believe it diminishes how their colleagues view them professionally. But the truth is that none of these are the real challenge. The real challenge is to override the discomfort we feel when we are exposed. Can we afford not to?

Revealing more of myself may not be easy, but I will give it some consideration. How will it feel to give others an opportunity to see another side of me? How will that benefit me and add to my work experience?

Working with an Attitude of Gratitude

When we think of our blessings, the gift of loved ones, both at home and at work, comes to mind. We are also grateful for everyone who has positively influenced our lives—our parents, children, friends, teachers, colleagues or neighbors.

When we think about our work, though, gratitude may not come immediately to mind. There are a lot of aspects of our work that we take for granted or that we simply don't pay much attention to, so they escape our consideration when we think about what we are grateful for. And, yet, a few moments of reflection can yield a long gratitude list. Hopefully, you work with colleagues who are dedicated to the care of others and you recognize the incredibly important mission of the work you do. Most employees recognize the quality of clinical care you deliver and would strongly recommend your facilities to family, friends and neighbors, not only as a place to receive quality care, but also as a place to work. Your organization may not be perfect, but it is intent on becoming the best.

In the midst of the demands of everyday life and the stresses of the work place, recognizing our blessings and developing a grateful heart might not seem important. To glimpse its value, simply find a moment to be quiet, recall your blessings, and then return to the work at hand. As Mother Teresa of Calcutta so beautifully stated, "I slept and I dreamed that life is all joy, I woke and I saw that life is all service. I served and I saw that service is joy." Simply reflecting on her words can create the dramatic shift in our perspective that we so desperately crave at certain points in our work day.

Individuals who live with grateful hearts don't experience a deep void that needs to be constantly filled by taking something from others. Instead, they find it easy to give. That change of attitude influences how we relate to others. Our patients will feel the difference. So will our colleagues. So will we.

I will practice having an attitude of gratitude. I will take time to reflect on my blessings and see how this changes how I feel about my work, and my life.

*E*mbracing *Feedback*

As managers, department heads or team leaders, there is a risk in sharing our goals for our organization with others. In doing so, we are publicly setting a high standard for the whole group for which we will be held accountable, and it can be disillusioning to get survey feedback that we didn't measure up to our own standards.

Surveys may confront us with an unpleasant reality—that patients are not satisfied with how they are being treated. They feel they were rushed, that mistakes were made, that their concerns weren't heard, that overall they weren't treated as individuals. It is embarrassing to acknowledge and even more discomforting to accept the idea that as much as we hold the desire to be caring and helpful, the incessant demands of the moment force us to drop our most important goal—the thoughtful, careful treatment of patients. One survey done at my own hospital showed that a surprising number of patients indicated that they did not receive "polite and professional" treatment. And yet this is precisely what we want to do.

What do you do when you are not pleased with the results of a survey? How do you take responsibility rather than merely harboring anger and disappointment?

You face it head on. One group of nurses in this hospital was so determined to change their patients' experience that they developed a campaign entitled "It's your mama in that bed." The phrase reminded them to treat everyone with particular sensitivity and as a whole person. In other words, they didn't just treat the condition.

The same principle applies when we interact with one another as colleagues. We need to be as sensitive to one another as those nurses were trying to be to their patients. If you think about how much a simple kind human gesture can mean to you, imagine how much it means to a patient who can barely take his next breath, who is in pain, or who is facing his own mortality.

Finding ways to be polite and professional with patients, their families, as well as with one another, is an important stepping stone to becoming the best at what we do. If you have discovered ways to create that attitude where you work—and if you believe that these will help others—pass your ideas on to them.

Today, I will embrace feedback as a great learning tool for improving the way I do my job. Using this information, I will creatively come up with a solution for better serving my patients and coworkers.

Earning Trust

Yesterday, I heard the highly respected Chief Financial Officer of a health care system known for its quality of care, tell a hundred of its leaders why he no longer trusts today's health care system. That statement got my attention! How could someone so knowledgeable of the inner workings of health care say such a thing? Because he knows that the pressure in today's health market to make medical institutions responsive to shareholder expectations often collides with, and sharply interferes with its primary purpose of creating an environment where healing takes place. Sometimes profit trumps people.

Patients know that hospitals are not run as charities. And, they know that paying the bill just comes with the territory—it's the price of receiving the latest technology and treatment from highly skilled, trained professionals. Nevertheless, they have to inherently trust that in spite of the money factor, our real motivation is the job, not the paycheck. They hope we care about what happens to them and that we'll go the extra mile to make sure that they are safe, comfortable, and nurtured back to health.

There are different levels of trust. In a family, it looks like one thing. "Tom," the CFO, said he was fortunate because, in his family, "we trust one another, and we know how to access medical care when we need it." Four of his siblings are physicians and share a common knowledge. Whenever someone in his family needs medical care, they all huddle before deciding on the next step. There is an implicit understanding that everyone holds the well being of their patient/family member in the highest regard. In our capacity as health care professionals, we need to be doing the same thing.

Our hospitals, treatment centers and offices might not be our families, yet, all health care is based on trusting that we put the patient first. The question we must ask ourselves is, "What do we have to do to earn our patients' trust?" People often think there is a complex, almost mystical answer to this, but actually, the answer is quite simple. We do it one task at a time. We accomplish it through all the small things we do every day to meet patients' needs. Every time we relieve a patient's suffering, bring her medication on time and respond promptly to his call button, trust grows a little more.

There are many, seemingly small things we can do that have great consequence. They require being doggedly attentive to the task at hand, whatever the job might be.

- If a lab technician, we can check and double-check our results.
- If a nurse, we can be single-minded about the accuracy of taking orders.
- If a physician, we can take the time to become uncanny listeners with sharpened observational skills. Many a complex diagnosis is decoded by listening "between the lines" to what our patient is telling us.
- If working within nutritional services, we can make sure that what we serve is what has been requested.
- If working within the business office, we can resolve billing issues in a timely and pleasant way.
- If an office assistant, we can make the extra effort to keep our department organized and on track.
- If a respiratory therapist, we can be sure we arrive on time to a patient's bedside and that our treatment is well documented in the chart.
- If an electrician, we can respond quickly to a call for help and solve the problem that could make a huge difference in the medical staff's day.

Why is all this important? Because, the caregiver who directly interacts with the patient can only be as good as those who work behind the scenes to support her activities. And, when the caregiver is careless and detached, the patient senses it. He learns to distrust all of us through this one act of callousness. Every one of our jobs is important and valued because if we do not pull together as an organization, we fail our patients.

Some may speak of hospitals as businesses, yet they are also places where people genuinely care about people in very specialized ways. The way we build trust—one act at a time—will profoundly impact our effectiveness as a business and as a place of healing.

What can I do today to improve the care that patients receive? Today, I will look for ways to earn the trust of others by consistently delivering the highest quality of work.

C*ourage to* S*peak*

I had the good fortune to volunteer behind the information table for a few hours yesterday afternoon. I thought that I was there to provide information, but I ended up receiving more than I gave.

The table is next to the hospital's front door, which is used by many patients after they are discharged. To provide easy entrance for others, patients in wheelchairs leaving the hospital sometimes wait directly in front of the table, which displays pictures and books dealing with loss and death, describing them as a normal part of living. It was noticeable how the patients sitting there would take a quick glance at the display and then look the other way.

One day, the eye of a patient caught mine. She smiled and I went over to say hello. "You know," she said, "I've noticed how people look away from the table. Most of us find it hard to speak about important things. Death is one of those things. We think we have to wait for the right time to say something. The fact is, there is never a right time. Now that I have cancer, I have learned not to wait to have a conversation. Real conversations begin when one person has the courage to speak."

Her words rung in my ears, "Real conversations only begin when one person has the courage to speak." We can learn a lot from our patients.

Death is a primary example of something we find hard to talk about, but in our every day work life, other topics that are in the air can be every bit as difficult, yet important, to speak up about. It is quite hard, for example, for patients to express their dissatisfaction to the staff because of a fear of "biting the hand that feeds them." So when they do open up enough to complain, we can listen.

We are inescapably interdependent on one another. When a patient feels unsafe or dissatisfied, it is everyone's responsibility to change the way the system works. No one can say, "It is their problem, not mine." Things will only change when one person has the courage to speak.

Don't let a potential conflict with a colleague stop you. Think of it as an opportunity for a real conversation—one that will only happen if you push through your resistance and bring the subject up.

Today, I will have the courage to speak up.

$\mathcal{A}$wakening to Our Lives

Both my mother and father died of heart failure. My siblings all seem to have inherited the same congenital heart problems. My older brother had a heart attack when he was fifty-seven years old, my younger brother had stents inserted when he was fifty-six, and my older sister had heart failure while skiing at Vail and has since had a valve replaced. Another sister had a stroke. I am the only one in my immediate family without known serious cardiac problems. That is unsettling because it reawakens my awareness of the finiteness of life.

When I was leaving the parking lot of a hospital one day, heading for a meeting in another, I drove out of a darkened underground garage. As soon as the automatic door opened, I was struck by the incredible beauty of the blue sky. The contrast was remarkable. Soon, I felt the welcome chill in the morning air and noticed children playing on the side of the road. I relished what I was observing. There is something about serious illness and being faced with our own vulnerability that puts things in perspective. We are awakened to the world.

The challenge in health care is to recognize the beauty and value of our work that is often masked by the ordinariness of everyday activities.

We often think of work as a task, yet it is also about awakening. When we are awakened, we work a little differently. Patients know the difference. Let us help one another live reflectively.

I will live my life today with a greater sense of awareness and appreciation of my life, my work and the people around me. I will strive to approach my life and work with more reflection. I will look at the beauty of life and creation and awaken to the gifts that surround me.

Remembering to Pause

We were indoors yesterday, busy in operating rooms, on floors, and at desks in windowless offices. Many cared for patients; many more worked in support of those who do. It is understandable that we may have forgotten that it was the first day of autumn.

Though busy, and as important as work is, it is also valuable to pause, if only for a moment, to remember our lives apart from work. As we stop and reflect, our thoughts will likely turn to our loved ones: children, parents, and friends. These moments are not a distraction. They are an invitation to see with fresh and appreciative eyes our loved ones, the beauty of this season, and most importantly, the beauty of those we serve. They are a reminder that we are participating in the mystery of life that always eludes pat answers and trouble-free explanations.

When we return to our homes, let's take a moment to recognize once again the love of our friends and the value of our work.

Today, I will take a break from work to reflect on events going on outside of my life, and be grateful for the friends and loved ones in my life. I will return to work with renewed energy and the desire to do my best.

Controlling the Future

On Groundhog Day, we learn whether Puxatawny Phil sees his shadow or not when he emerges from his winter home in the hills of Pennsylvania. Is winter over yet?

Groundhog Day is a metaphor for the ways in which we look for hints about how the future will unfold. Who has not wondered about the rest of their child's life or the length of one's days? Of course, no one has total control of the future. Wars, earthquakes, accidents, and unexpected illnesses are proof enough. It is the wise person, then, who lives every moment with an attitude of gratitude.

The best way to predict the future is to shape it by what we do today. We all have a vision of what we want to happen. If you make it your goal to strive for excellence, to be part of an organization that excels in care, and to be of service to your patients, to become the best—and you work toward that goal daily—then you will be preparing for it to occur. Today's actions create the future.

Every person in the organization is involved in this process. While our responsibilities may vary, what we do, or do not do as individuals and as teams, shape patient care.

Think about how much greater the impact on our organizations will be if we model this behavior as a team, and if everyone on the team works together daily to accomplish the same goal. If that common vision is to work as a team—or a collection of teams—to provide the best patient care, medical errors will drop, patient satisfaction will increase, and the delivery of high-quality patient care will be assured. Looking at it from this perspective, we can see that together, we have a much better chance of predicting the future than Puxatawny Phil.

The actions I take today will influence the future. While I cannot predict this outcome, I can control what I do by being aware of my actions and doing my best.

Making a Resolution to Believe in Change

As we close out one year and begin a new one, most of us make New Year's resolutions. Some of us resolve to spend more time with our families or to change the way we work. We may resolve to eat healthier or to exercise more regularly. Whatever the *re-solution*, it is generally associated with re-solving a recurring problem.

Some no longer make New Year's resolutions. Remembering how ineffectual our past efforts were, we have become a little jaded. But don't just assume you should resign yourself to the status quo just because your attempts to change didn't work. Even if in the past, you tried and tried and nothing changed, or you were unable to fix your wayward behavior, it is not because change is impossible. Upon closer examination, you may find that some change did take place, just not to the degree you had hoped. Change, especially when it requires a huge shift in values, actions or long-held attitudes, occurs in baby steps; sometimes they're so small that they are hardly noticeable at first. Or, maybe your initial expectations were too high, but if you reflect more closely on your efforts, you'll see that you've made real progress toward your goal. Did you write off the whole endeavor because you were successful for a while, but then back-pedaled or stalled out? Did you set a goal that required someone or something to change that was outside of your control?

Whatever conclusion you come to after looking at past disappointments, don't let those setbacks keep you from trying. Why? Because the alternative is to become stuck in your life and accepting of what you've already determined is unacceptable. Once we begin to believe that it is useless to try to change, we atrophy.

If even a small part of you is still open to inspiration and the idea that change is possible, then you can't give up on yourself or on the world, which will benefit from your growth and accomplishment. Rather than giving up altogether, look back on where you fell short and why. It may be because of a simple reason, or it may be that this change couldn't have worked last year, but could work this year.

What happens to individuals can also happen to groups. When organizations become jaded, employees disengage and grow helpless because they believe the future will just be an extension of the past. They lose their incentive to change and blame others for the team's failures. Accountability goes out the window, virtually guaranteeing a downward slide and a miserable environment for everyone.

Change starts with a desire within ourselves. We don't need to wait until New Year's to make a resolution. We can resolve to take a new step toward changing a behavior every day. We can start over in the middle of a day. We can always choose to begin again.

Today, I will make a small change in my personal or work life. I will follow through with that change each day and be a powerful force for change in my work place.

Giving the Gift of Life

Many of us who are in health care contribute to the field in ways that extend beyond any paycheck or job description. Everyone who donates blood helps people they will never meet, but who will be eternally grateful for their life-saving gift. I know of one employee, Dan, who has participated in the blood donor program 150 times! The platelets he donates each month are valued at several hundred dollars per unit, yet he receives no money at all for it; he does it because he knows how important it is. The total monetary value of his contribution to patients is estimated to be over $100,000 dollars. Can you imagine the lives saved and number of successful surgeries enhanced by his generosity? In my mind, this kind of selfless act makes Dan a saint, yet he remains in the background. The world is a better place because of him.

Many employees in health care make this important pilgrimage each month; some have donated platelets or plasma over a hundred times. Even retired employees return to donate. It takes about an hour to give plasma, about two for platelets, and the value far outweighs the inconvenience.

Everyday, we walk around with this amazing gift that our bodies produce continuously. What better way to express gratitude for our own health than by sharing this "liquid gold" with others.

Can I find time to donate blood? I will look for ways to enrich my life by helping others.

How We Work, Not What We Do

Over the holidays one of our employees, Janet, died unexpectedly. She was only in her early thirties, a wife and mother of two, and worked in Accounts Payable. She was a warm, vibrant, and engaged woman. It's not uncommon for employees in Accounts Payable to have contact with the rest of us only by phone. Outside of Janet's own department, no one really knew her, except by her pleasant voice. Most of us hadn't even met her face-to-face. Yet, at the service, person after person stood up to speak about their cherished relationship with this woman. I couldn't help thinking, "How can so many different individuals with such varied backgrounds feel that they had a special relationship with a woman they hadn't actually met?" As one person remarked, even the neighborhood dogs found their way to her home! Why? Because of her warm and magnetic personality.

Every one of us brings more than just competence to our work. What makes each of us memorable to those around us is our very presence. Janet's life was a gift to us, and a reminder that how we do our job is just as important as the job we do. When Janet answered the phone or greeted someone, we walked away feeling seen, heard and cared about. When you die, how will you be remembered? Others will think of us not so much by what we did or said, but by how we made them feel about themselves. Let us return to our work renewed and motivated by this heightened perspective to treat others in a deeper, more meaningful way with every phone call we make, every email we send, each hand we shake, and every shoulder we touch.

I will take time today to reflect on the legacy I am creating. I can shape that legacy through every day interactions at work and at home.

$\mathcal{T}$hrough the Eyes of a Child

There was a lot of buzz about the upcoming employee picnic at the zoo. On the day before the picnic, I was standing next to an employee waiting for a meeting to begin, and I asked her, "Are you going to the zoo tomorrow?" "I am," she said, "but I'm disappointed. I wanted to take my niece. She's six years old and has never been to a zoo. A few days ago she fell and bruised herself badly and can't walk very well. I'll miss her excitement, particularly because she would be seeing so many things for the first time."

Her words about missing the thrill of going with a child stayed with me during the entire time I was at the zoo. Perhaps because I was alone so I wasn't drawn into adult conversations, my attention kept being pulled toward the kids and at how excited they really were to see the animals. Their curiosity was undeniable. I watched a particularly determined little girl convince her mother that it was okay to touch the animals in the petting area. The pleasure she found in stroking the lambs was unquestionable.

Why is it more fun to go to the zoo with children? Is it because their enthusiasm, curiosity and excitement are contagious? Is it because, as adults, that side of ourselves, which we often overlook, is awakened again by their antics?

All of us have a childlike wonder and curiosity buried within. Some of us have kept our carefree, spirited selves under layers of a self-imposed sense of duty and seriousness, believing that there is no place for light-hearted "unproductive" activities. This group feels that those childish ways and days are behind them and the life of a responsible adult has no room for play or taking off on a lark. Others are able to more effortlessly liberate this childlike enthusiasm and excitement by engaging in activities that they loved as children, be it flying a kite, playing a pick-up game of basketball, singing in a choir or getting their hands dirty in a moist lump of modeling clay. Then there are those who, while holding down serious jobs or having earned great credibility and respect in their communities, seem to balance that with an easy sense of joy and wonder at the simple events that take place in daily life. They revel at sunrises, take in the full aroma of a freshly brewed cup of coffee, and can't wait to play an impromptu game of catch with a neighbor's dog and a found tennis ball. This group of people seems to squeeze every moment out of life, making each day a pleasure and thus becoming a magnet, drawing in those around them who hope that some of this magic will rub off.

All of us have the capacity to tap into the childlike wonder that resides within us. When we grow comfortable with being curious and enthusiastic at work, we not only feel better, but we become more engaged and better healers. We become far more innovative in dealing with ambiguity. More than likely, others find it easier to be with us, too. Care is enhanced when we have a simplicity that sees the world as if for the first time.

We, like children, are seeing things for the first time all the time. Whenever a physician or nurse meets a new patient, they are seeing someone for the first time. Every time we see an unfamiliar employee walking towards us in the hallway, or sitting beside us at a meeting, we are having a first-time experience.

Do you think clinical outcomes can be affected if a physician sees his patients as if for the first time? Do you think that we feel differently when others look at us in fresh ways? The real question is can we, whatever our professions or responsibilities, be mature enough to let children teach us?

Today, I will approach my work with wonder and newness by embracing first-time experiences. I will look for a new way of doing my job and bring a sense of excitement and joy into my work.

$\mathcal{T}$ransforming Failure

We often think of failure as something that we should avoid at all costs. Do you think this is a helpful way to think? Consider these two examples.

Thomas Edison once said he was grateful for the thousand failed experiments that led to his discovery of how to make the first light bulb. Not once did he view them as unnecessary or a waste of his time.

A master martial arts teacher tells his students that they cannot learn if they always win. Why? Because failure prompts closer examination of the problem, it spurs them to make a greater effort to win the next time, and it inspires innovation, which will lead to an even better performance in the future. The trick is to not become stuck in the failure, endlessly berating oneself for the mistakes. Mistakes are not outside the process; they are part of the process.

How does this principle of failure relate to those of us who are working at the bedside of patients, running tests in windowless labs, reading films, filling prescriptions, preparing meals or doing detail work in out-of-the-way cubicles? We can only become the best at what do if we appreciate failure and realize that it is essential to any success.

Failure is a part of life. How we deal with it separates the cautious from the creative, as individuals, teams, and organizations.

Today, I will be more committed to learning and growing professionally and personally through the exposure and examination of my failures. New ideas will result from this courageous approach.

Fighting Prejudice Through Self-Reflection

The late Coretta Scott King started out as a support for her husband, then became a force in her own right. She used her life to speak out resolutely about the need to love one another—regardless of ethnicity, religion or social standing. She told us how she herself kept this vision of love, in spite of her husband's violent death, which was brought about by racism. She accomplished this by having "...a commitment to rigorous self-analysis and self-criticism about the way we treat people." In her opinion, self-assessment inevitably leads to facing and naming our prejudice. The light of awareness alone often leads to prejudice dissolving because under close scrutiny, we realize that what we have in common is our fundamental humanity. We can almost envision a society in which everyone is valued. The problem, she thought, was that we were hesitant to look at ourselves and our ways honestly.

Coretta King's death is one more invitation to take a critical look at ourselves and discern the obstacles that keep us from seeing that we are all part of the human family. While she believed that individuals and groups were hesitant to do such probing, I suspect that we in health care are less timid. I have watched teams, departments and organizations work just as hard to save a homeless person as they would an heiress.

A test of our resolve to rid ourselves of prejudice and inequity is as close as the next moment we answer a phone or touch a patient or pass a stranger in the hallway. We can make this connection even with a perfect stranger if we approach him with heartfelt attention and caring. How was Coretta King able to show such warmth to the people she didn't know?

She took the inward trip and looked at herself honestly. What she saw was that others are in need of love as much as she. There is something heroic in that discovery.

Today, I will look honestly at my prejudices and biases. I will look beyond appearances today to the connection that everyone is yearning to feel from one another.

$\mathcal{K}$eeping Life from Getting in the Way

"Are you going to the hospital's Christmas dinner this year?"

"I was going to, but now I can't afford to take the time. And if I do show up, I probably can't stay. I've got too much to do."

I overheard that conversation the week before Christmas. The irony is that during these gatherings, we have the opportunity to socialize with our coworkers in a more personal way. These times are just as important as the time we spend working with them. Christmas parties are anything but frivolous; they build trust. So when you do find yourself in the operating room with that colleague the next day—the person you just shared an eggnog with the night before—the intuitive understanding you've built is working for you.

"I've been trying to reach you for days. I only need about five minutes."

"I'm swamped, let's set something up."

How often have we heard this kind of exchange?

When we are busy, it is easy to lose focus, become scattered, and consequently ineffective. Task-driven thinking will lead us to believe that someone asking us a question or going to a Christmas party are "distractions" and "interruptions." In fact, these are as integral to our work as the next item on our to-do list. Almost all of us have learned, yet forget, Alfred D'Souza's self-reflection:

For a long time it had seemed to me that life was about to begin—real life. But there was always some obstacle in the way, something to be got through first, some unfinished business, time still to be served, a debt to be paid. Then life would begin. At last it dawned on me that these obstacles were my life.

We are the ones who think of new requests, unexpected telephone calls, uninvited emails, and unscheduled meetings as interruptions rather than the stuff of life. The poet Blake reminds us that the tree that moves some to tears of joy is, in the eyes of others, a green thing that stands in their way of where they want to go!

Today, I will embrace unexpected events and be open to their blessing and opportunity, rather than see them as obstacles. I will see the unexpected as a gift and not let my life pass me by.

Managing Fear

The world, including our nation, has endured an incredible loss of life through the actions of terrorists. The unique hallmark of terrorism is that no one knows if, when or how violence will strike. That is what makes these times so frightening.

We know that when we walk through the doors at work, we must set aside many of the personal concerns that will interfere with our ability to be attentive to our patients.

Overly cautious and suspicious individuals do not make helpful caregivers. We need to show unconditional compassion for everyone. The challenge for all of us at this time in history is to recognize our insecurities, dampen our suspicions, and go beyond our immediate urge to be on guard, by reaching out with warmth and care.

Within health care, we pledge to foster the healing and health of those entrusted to us. That is our mission. It is not a vague, amorphous task. It is a practical attitude that can be applied every single day.

Today, I will set aside my vague fears of mistrust and uncertainty. I will focus on the very real task at hand of being a healing presence to those who come into my life today.

Creating Ceremonies

An employee asked if I would preside at her wedding. I laughed at what seemed an unusual request. "Of course not! I'm not a rabbi, priest, deacon, pastor or civil servant. I can't do that!" She was pleasantly assertive. "Sure you can. In this state, all you need is a lawyer and a license. We have that. We just want a meaningful ceremony for ourselves, loved ones, and friends." I sat on the decision for a time before saying okay. While this type of role is way outside of my comfort zone, I am glad that I agreed to do it.

The two wanted a public ceremony, one that was significant for them, and that would formally usher them into their new life together with the endorsement and support of family and friends. They knew there would be joyous as well as dark times ahead, and making their commitment public was a way of gaining support for whatever the future held.

My involvement in their wedding prompted me to ask myself what role ceremony plays in our work lives. Just as in our personal lives, in health care, we have joyous as well as challenging times ahead. We also share our many hours at work with our coworkers—not in as intimate a way as this couple, but we are similarly engaged in a shared commitment to provide the best possible clinical care and service. Are there ceremonies that we can create in our work setting that help us stay together when we want to give up?

Why are ceremonies important? Because they touch a side of life that words alone will never reach. Think of it this way. For those in love, there is a time for words; there is another time for a kiss upon awakening. To forget about the role of ceremony in our lives is to live narrowly.

Try to recall a past ceremony that was particularly meaningful. Once you remember one, think about the how it changed you or those who participated. With thoughtful reflection, you will see their value in changing people from the inside out, and in turn changing the culture where we work, from the inside out.

Today, I will think about the role that ceremonies have played in unifying my personal community at key moments in my life. How have those events helped during dark times? How can I add ceremonies that will deepen my team's commitment to one another and to our work?

Slowing Down and Thinking About All We Have

Today, let's take some time to think about how we work. For many of us, taking time to reflect—even for a few minutes—feels like a luxury we just can't afford. It's easy to walk through the doors at work and get swept up in the demands coming at us from all sides, almost simultaneously. And yet, taking time for reflection before or even during our work day can create a vital shift in our attitude, open us to unexpected answers to nagging problems, inspire a new approach to treating a patient or coworker—in other words, enliven our work lives with a renewed energy and even generosity of spirit. The health benefits of reflection or meditation are widely known: lowered blood pressure, improved heart rate and the other positive physical effects that we feel when we take steps to lower our stress. It's worthwhile and practical to give ourselves the gift of time. One place to start is to cultivate an attitude of gratitude.

Each day we have a chance to recognize our blessings. Is your stomach full? Do you live in a real home? Are you free to pursue your own kind of happiness? For those who have grown up with these gifts, it is so easy to take them for granted. But it's important to realize that millions of people across the globe do not have these basics. When we feel grateful, we want to share our good fortune with others. In the East, they have a saying: giving something away "creates an empty space" for something new to come into your life. When we carry the awareness of abundance into our work, we will see occasions to express gratitude all around us. The opportunity is as immediate as the stranger walking toward us, the patient in the next room, or our colleague in the neighboring cubicle.

While no work place is perfect, many of us are blessed to have valuable jobs and pleasant working conditions. It only takes a moment to recognize that most of the things we complain about are small compared to our blessings.

I will slow down and take time to reflect on all of the gifts in my life. I will carry this attitude into all that I do and see how opportunities arise that enrich my experience and the lives of those I meet.

Standing in a Moment of Opportunity

On Inauguration Day our President places his right hand on a Bible, raises his hand in a gesture to express the solemn nature of what he is about to do, and then voices an oath, not simply a promise.

Inauguration Day is "gap-like" time. As a community, we stand in a moment between what was, is, and what will be. Today, something new is beginning. The future holds the secret of what that will be.

You and I provide health care to those in need. We will not be elected President and we will never know the consequences of taking the Oath of Office. However, every time we meet a patient, speak to their families, prepare their medications, clean rooms, ready meals, order supplies, review charts, check bills or work on spreadsheets, we stand in a moment of opportunity.

How we do what we do will shape the future. In some ways, our opportunities to fashion this sacred world are no less frequent than those of our President.

I will take a moment to be quiet in the midst of this workday. I will realize the power I have to shape my day.

$\mathcal{A}$pplying New Ideas to Our Work

When people go away for conferences, they often return excited and re-energized because they've been exposed to a great many ideas that enlightened and inspired them. Have you ever returned from a conference only to realize that others are not as moved as you are when you relate your experience? Then you think, "Of course not, they're getting it second-hand. Besides, how could I or anyone reduce those hours of learning into a ten-minute conversation?"

There is an oft-quoted phrase within Rabbinic, Muslim and Christian traditions: "Preach always. Use words if you must." What this means is that the words, themselves, no matter how well executed, are not as formative as the whole experience. It's how we apply what we've learned that will demonstrate the value of what we learned from any conference or training.

When we are at work, it is helpful to remember that *how* we work speaks to others in remarkably powerful ways.

Today, I will look for ways to apply what I've learned at conferences to my everyday work. I'm grateful to have had this training and I will express my gratitude in the new way I approach my work.

Grief as Teacher

Grief often teaches us how to live. A colleague mentioned to me that when her dog died, her daughter was distraught. The night before he died, the daughter had yelled at him to get out of the kitchen and stop bothering her. "If I knew he was ill and was going to die, I would never have yelled." That is another way of saying that she would have lived a little differently had she realized that he was going to die.

From personal experience, I will never forget the look on my mother's face when I walked out of her hospital room for the last time. My sisters and I were leaving to catch a bite to eat, but while we were gone she slipped into a coma. The following morning she died. If I had known, I would have stayed and expressed my love for the last time.

These examples may seem sentimental. They are not. They are simply every day examples of the way in which awareness of the fragile nature of life invites us to live a little differently, live with a more immediate recognition that life's continuity is far from guaranteed and its direction can change course in a flash.

For some people, it takes a death to jolt them out of their complacency that life will go on no matter what. Whatever strengthens our appreciation of life—including grief—will help us treat our patients and colleagues in increasingly sensitive ways.

Today, I will be aware of how fragile life is. I will use this awareness of the fragility of life to help me make good choices in my interactions with others.

Needing to Connect

Reflect on what many individuals did when they were trapped on the upper floors of the burning World Trade Center. Passengers on the hijacked airliner did the same. So did those running from collapsing buildings when they reached a doorway or safe spot. They called home.

Today, answering machines preserve their recorded calls. "I don't know what's happening. I'm scared. Know that I love you." Those recordings are now saved and kept in safe places in an effort to hold onto the last cherished words of loved ones.

Buried within our hearts, less deeply than we might imagine, is a profound need to be connected and to express our love.

When entering a hospital or when preoccupied with an unknown or feared condition, patients have sentiments similar to those expressed on 9/11. In the face of death, it's not their account balance they want to see, it's the faces of those they love.

I will remember the voices of 9/11 and how they instinctively needed to connect with loved ones when I think of the patients I may meet today.

Having Good Humor

Yesterday, I was speaking with an employee who, for thirty years, worked in the hospital's food services department. She had recently suffered a heartbreaking experience and she wanted to talk to me about it. Her daughter and her 7-year-old granddaughter had been struck by a car while crossing the street. The daughter had internal injuries that left her out of work for six months, and her granddaughter suffered serious spinal cord injuries resulting in a paralysis of her legs. This vibrant, happy, and energetic soccer player would no longer be able to walk. The employee described the stress and strain this had placed on the entire family as they coped with the little girl's tragedy and the financial burden of a lost income from the mother.

After bearing her soul in the most touching way, she stopped, and with tears still on her cheeks, she smiled, tipped her head upward, and said, "I'm blessed." I knew what this meant. In spite of her devastating experience, she still managed to be grateful for all the good things she still had in her life. I have no idea how she had developed this disposition during a life that was touched by recurring and significant pain, but she did. When she left my office, I had the lingering feeling that I had just met a thoroughly genuine and resilient person with an appreciative attitude toward life. Some of us are graced with a buoyancy that lets us weather life's ups and downs with an optimistic attitude, which, in ancient times used to be referred to as "good humors."

The ancients believed that the nature of "humors" within us gave us our temperaments. For instance, one blend of humors gave individuals a sanguine (upbeat) temperament; other mixtures made individuals have phlegmatic (calm) or choleric (excitable) temperaments. Today, we think of "good" humored individuals as those who are optimistic, positive and cheerful. An "ill" humored person is one who cannot tolerate misfortune without being thrown off base. This employee certainly fell in the former category.

A good-humored staff, whether the attitude comes naturally or whether they have to work for it, helps to create a healing climate for patients. But, there is a challenge. We don't always wake up with good humor. Even if we do, we can lose it in the midst of the day's activities. Neither our patients nor our colleagues deserve our bad humor. So, as odd as it seems, we must learn to "pretend" in an honest way. This kind of pretense is not false; it is a manifestation of the respect we have toward others. Being able to put our feelings behind us is a mark of maturity.

Today, I will bring a positive, open attitude to my work. When I'm feeling down, I'll take a moment apart to regain perspective. I'm here for others.

*E*mbracing Diversity During the Holidays

The holiday season represents a unique time of year when many of us publicly display and express our religious beliefs. During the rest of the year, we often keep these beliefs to ourselves and practice our traditions within our religious communities. There is something about the shortened days of winter and the traditions associated with the winter holidays—decorating our homes with festive lights and exchanging gifts— that makes this public expression and celebration of our moral and religious values uniquely acceptable this time of year.

Remarkably, many of the world's greatest religions and traditions celebrate their important day at the same time of the year. Christians celebrate Christmas, Chanukah begins for the Jewish people and African Americans celebrate Kwanzaa.

Christians think of this holiday as the season in which they rejoice in their belief that God has entered this world. They consider this creation as sacred.

Chanukah is the time when Jews remember celebrating the victory over religious oppression to finally practice their religion as they chose. The miracle of a flame lasting eight days when there was only enough oil to light the lamp for one day, confirmed their belief that G-d was with them, despite continued persecution through the centuries.

When African Americans celebrate Kwanzaa, they reaffirm their rich and varied cultures, as well as their memory and indebtedness to their ancestors, who paid an incredible price for freedom.

Holidays remind us of the need to acknowledge the sacredness of life and allow this awareness to influence how we live and work.

Today, I will embrace our differences and not be afraid of them. I will learn more about other traditions and discover our similarities while honoring our differences.

$\mathcal{L}$osing Perspective from Overwork

Our jobs have an intensity about them! To keep balance, we have to have a satisfying personal life apart from work. Without balance, everything at work can seem like a crisis.

Chronic overwork is the phenomenon of spending too much time working. For some that may be 12 hours a day; for others, four hours is too much. This is a growing American problem but it has always been an issue in health care.

A hospital is a high-stress environment to begin with, and overwork just throws fuel on the flame. Tempers flare more quickly, impulsive decisions are made, we overreact, and teamwork and the quality of care suffer. When many people work side by side under this much stress, it distorts the way they interact with others, and unfortunately, molehills turn into mountains. Yet within the work place, overwork can seem normal simply because everyone does it.

The challenge is not to find more vacation time (although that may be necessary), but to find a way to live a balanced life in the midst of everyday responsibilities.

Working more doesn't mean I'm working better. Others can fill in for me. The quality of my work will improve as I find a balance.

Taking Pride in Your Work

JCAHO recently rewarded us with incredibly high scores for patient safety and high clinical quality and service. And, not long ago, our hospital was named one of the nation's 100 Top Hospitals®. This is the eleventh time one of our hospitals has received this recognition. We are justly proud of these accomplishments, and yet, for our sake and the sake of our organization, we must step back and think about what kind of pride we are feeling and what we are going to do with it.

Let's go with the idea that there are two kinds of pride: "good" pride and "bad" pride. We may be quick to label pride as a "bad" thing in part because we hear it referred to as one of the seven deadly sins. The sinful kind is borne of arrogance, or full-of-oneself puffery that results in being blinded to shortcomings and potential pitfalls. Consumed by this kind of pride, people assume an attitude of being so perfect that there's no room for improvement, no need to get input from others. Before long, complacency sets in. Arrogant pride also breeds a feeling of superiority, fed by an unhealthy competition and need to compare, which greatly diminishes one's ability to work as a team or unite around achieving new goals as an organization. They are headed toward a cliff and don't see it coming because they're too busy patting themselves on the back. Remember the biblical phrase, "pride goeth before the fall."

But, there is such a thing as good pride. When we experience an accomplishment that fills us with "good" pride, we are pleased with the outcome itself, rather than what it says about us. This prideful feeling is tempered with a dose of humility and self-reflection, which leads us to experience a sense of accomplishment that is grounded in the knowledge that there's also room for improvement. Unhealthy competition and comparison have no place here, since we don't have the need to steal the spotlight and lay claim to the achievement. It allows us to see that our accomplishment is the product of good teamwork, not a reflection of our superiority.

At this institution, are we proud in the sense that we can boast on billboards around the city that we are the city's best hospital? Of course not. We are, however, rightfully pleased with our accomplishments.

The genius pianist, Vladimir Horowitz was intensely proud, and yet he was also critical of himself. When he was about to receive a Lifetime Achievement Award for being the most accomplished pianist of the last century, he was asked why he never smiled after playing. He replied, "I see what others don't. My playing has to improve. I'm driven to improve. Why smile when something is not the way it needs to be?" The kind of pride we strive for is the type artisans have when they take enormous pleasure in the outcome of all the effort they put in and the skill level they have achieved. And yet, this feeling is not the domain of artists or "special" people, an idea that the culture particularly supports. Our society constantly tells us that athletes and entertainers are our most important citizens. If you eliminate them for a week however, society wouldn't fall apart. Try eliminating farmers, sanitation workers, nurses, LPNs, housekeepers, dietary staff or lab technicians. Society would fall apart.

Whatever job you have in the health care system, it is essential. Your pride comes from the fact that what you do is valuable and necessary. Your job contributes to the hospital's reputation for high quality. When someone works hard to clean and polish the floor of a busy corridor and then overhears a visitor commenting on the cleanliness of the hospital, that's a cause for honest pride. It is the sentiment that an office assistant has when she is satisfied with the way she writes an errorless letter. We are appreciative of the billing clerk's talent to catch errors before bills are sent.

We are not pianists, athletes or actors, yet we are all artists in our own way. We can realize the value of the work we do, acknowledge our achievements, be grateful for the recognition we receive, celebrate it and push on.

Can I take pride in my work and in my organization?

The Impact of Working with Soul

The quality of our work is measured one interaction at a time. Its value is determined as much by how we work as it is by what we actually do. If our work is performed in a soul-less, mechanical way, its quality is diminished, along with our experience. But, by creating a conscious intention of connecting with patients and coworkers, we enhance our experience, as well as the care we provide. The quality of our work improves.

All of us know colleagues who demonstrate a unique ability to make a lasting impact on those they serve. If they performed like robots with the intention of just getting the job done, they would not likely have left an impression.

People who infuse their work with soul give each person, with each interaction, a piece of themselves, and that piece enriches the lives of both giver and receiver. It would seem that if they kept giving and giving and giving of themselves, there would be nothing left. Ironically, these people end the day feeling fulfilled, not empty. Those who work in this way are left with a feeling of accomplishment and a day well lived.

Many religious and spiritual beliefs are rooted in the notion that when we act with selflessness, we expand in energy and awareness. When we receive without giving, we actually contract. The Dead Sea, when thought of as a metaphor, illustrates this point. Typical lakes are teeming with marine life. This is only possible because of the continual inflow and outflow of nutrient-rich rivers and streams. It's not enough for there to just be an inflow. The vitality of these lakes is just as dependent on the outflow of the rivers, because they allow for an interaction of spawning fish in addition to flushing out waste and other matter. All of this works in an exquisitely balanced ecosystem. The Dead Sea, however, has no outflow. Only the Jordon River feeds it, with no rivers or streams leaving it. As a result of having no outlet for "giving away" its water, the Dead Sea has such a high salt content that it cannot support any life, thus the name, Dead Sea.

Whether in a cubical, windowless office, lab, or bedside, our work is, in and of itself, both necessary and valuable. Whatever your job, you are going to have an impact on the people around you and on your organization as a whole. The question is what kind of impact do you want to have? How you perform your job presents you with the opportunity to transform it into an authentic expression of the desire to heal and contribute to a cohesive, supportive and productive environment. The people who work with soul motivate us and show us how to relate to one another and to our patients in welcoming ways.

Today, I will be aware of how I do my job. I will focus on how I can contribute to all with whom I come in contact. I will enjoy my work more as I function with a soulful intention.

Having a Lasting Impact

Recently, I was involved in two seemingly unrelated meetings. What they both illustrated was the powerful ripple effect of our everyday words and actions not only on the people we treat, but on the overall functioning of our organization. The first was with a communications executive who was asked where she planned to budget her scarce financial resources: on an advertising campaign to the community promoting the positive things happening at the hospitals, or on internal communications projects? Without hesitating, she responded, "The best advertisements for the hospitals are its employees." She explained that good external advertising campaigns can be very effective in bolstering community support for our hospitals. However, internal projects that lead to greater employee satisfaction and bolster morale and belief in the value of their work have a subtle but even more powerful impact in shaping our hospital's reputation in the community. With each positive employee/patient interaction, our reputation in the community is slowly enhanced. As these experiences accumulate, they become the most powerful public relations campaign we could ever have.

Each one of us has the power, through our words and actions, to create a cumulative wave of good will, raising our community's perception of us and building up our hospital's reputation.

If you don't think we can have this kind of monumental impact, consider this. A week after my meeting with this communications executive, I met a former patient of ours who, twelve years ago, had been hospitalized for more than a month following surgery. A few weeks after his first operation, he had to undergo a second one. Today, he is in good health and in his mid-fifties. What few people know is that after he fully recovered, he started coming to the hospital for three hours, every week, and has been doing so for the past ten years. No, not for treatment, but to volunteer as a Patient Visitor on the same floor where he had been a patient so many years earlier. Why does he do this? Out of sheer gratitude to those who cared for him.

The communications executive was coming from an advertising and public relations perspective. Her statement was a reminder that every single employee is an ambassador for an institution. In addition to that, our words and behaviors outside of work subtly shape the community's perception also. The appreciative patient is a reminder of how influential we are in patients' lives. Each of us, wherever we work and whatever we do, can build a better world. We are more influential than we might imagine.

I will be aware of the lives I'm influencing. I will be an ambassador for healing as I touch others' lives. This awareness adds meaning to my work and to my personal life.

$\mathcal{E}$xpressing Our Inner Lives

A physician who had just run the Boston Marathon told me that he had originally planned to use his cell phone to call friends during the 26 mile race. "After all," he quipped, "I had three hours on my hands!"

However, once he began to run, he changed his mind. In the long tradition of runners, he decided to write someone's name in large letters all over his shirt. The name he picked was that of his son, Michael, who had died in a sporting accident the year before. The physician chose to run in his boy's honor.

He spoke of what it felt like to have spectators notice his son's name as they cheered him on. They were yelling out, "Go for it! Run for Michael!" Words couldn't convey what it felt like to run for, and with, his son. No wonder he decided not to use his cell phone. It would have been an interruption of the deeper experience of this event. Instead of the three hours being empty space, they turned out to be an expression of his love for his child.

His first inclination was to fill the void. Instead, in an unforeseen moment, he decided to tuck the phone away and be with the void. How many of us don't tune into ourselves because we want to steer clear of the void? Either we're afraid of it or we think we'll be bored. Until we slow down, get quiet, and openly listen to the soulful voice within, we will miss the richness of our inner lives. By choosing to take in the real meaning of this marathon, the physician's experience was memorable. It changed what he saw and how he lived.

Our inner life needs time to be nourished, time for reflection. Some people meditate, others find a spot in nature to dwell, while some people simply use the opportunity of the traditional morning cup of coffee to find a few moments of silence. Our inner life is difficult to describe and even more challenging to measure. Tuning into it shapes how we see the world. If we take a more contemplative approach to life and work, our interactions change, the quality of our focus improves, and our interpretation of people's words and actions are less judgmental. It is our choice to bring our inner life to work or to leave it at home.

Today, I will nourish my inner life with time for reflection. My inner life will enrich my work experience and the lives of other if I let it.

Taking a Fresh Look at Our Life and Our Work

We usually think of time as a commodity. One moment adds to another in linear fashion. When in linear time, we generally think in terms of past, present, and the future. As we become a little older, time becomes a commodity with less and less remaining. We spend it wisely.

Time is also cyclical. Holidays, birthdays, and anniversaries, reoccur yearly. So do seasons. We find comfort in their predictability. Cyclical time awakens memory. That is why it is so important. It is the kind of time that reminds us that life is never finished.

Think of wedding anniversaries. They are opportunities to turn toward one another in fresh ways. Couples are grateful for what has been but they are also challenged to break free from the patterns that bind them, and to express what has not yet been expressed. This process deepens the relationship and makes life together stronger. Cyclical time has a way of pushing us beyond ourselves. Issues and problems never go away just because we work on them once. It may seem as if we have reached resolution, but there's always another dimension that hasn't been explored. "I thought I was done with that problem!" It may seem as if we are back where we started but in fact, we're now approaching it from a higher point. It's like following a circular path around and up a mountain. Every few hours, we find ourselves facing east again. The novice will think, "I haven't gotten anywhere." But the mature one realizes, "I'm a thousand feet higher!" Cyclical time helps us become wiser.

The routine of health care can be extremely repetitive. It can wear us down, causing us to err.

How do we avoid that? It starts with the recognition that we are tired. Next, we can pull back for a time and remember what we treasure about our jobs. These are fragile moments and need to be nourished. They support our dreams about our sense of mission. When we are true to ourselves, work is always more fulfilling; a full expression of who we are.

Today, I will get in touch with what motivated me to get into health care. I will think about how work nourishes me and renew my personal commitment to my sense of mission as expressed through what I do.

*I*D Tags and "Uniforms" as Symbols of Our Professional Ideals

Work may seem routine, but if we take a closer look, it is quite extraordinary. To glimpse its significance, consider something as simple as our identification tags, scrubs or white coats. They signal to our patients what we do. They establish our credentials and proficiency and reassure them that the person treating them is competent to do so. For someone who is ill, the signs are reassuring.

All of us need symbols. They help us understand what words cannot. A stole, for example is a symbol that indicates that the person wearing it has special authority. Magistrates, judges, and ministers wear this piece of cloth over their shoulders when they perform their duties. The symbol reminds those wearing it of their professional responsibilities and commitment. It awakens them to the need to live up to the highest standards of their profession. For those they serve, the stole confers authority and a degree of trustworthiness.

A badge is another symbol. When policemen wear the badge, it means they have particular responsibilities entrusted to them by society. Similar to priests and rabbis, they are part of something larger than themselves.

You and I wear symbols. While we do not wear stoles or badges, we do wear scrubs, white coats, and employee identification tags that communicate to others that we are representatives of the medical profession and of our hospital. People confer authority on us, and it is up to us to live up to the trust they place in us.

Our health care organization has no face other than you and I.

My ID tag or uniform is a symbol of my commitment to the profession of healing. When I put on my ID tag or uniform, I am showing others and reminding myself that I am committed to the ideals of my profession.

Slowing Down and Feeling Grateful

When we are busy, health care can seem like it is merely a job. There are procedures to follow, policies to implement, rooms to ready, charts to review, walls to paint, bills to send, prescriptions to fill, materials to purchase, and patients to discharge. It's no wonder we are in a rush.

When we slow down, it gives us the chance to appreciate the fact that we are people caring for people. Our work place serves as a unique environment for demonstrating something intangible about life, love, service, and caring. Not only do we express our best qualities in the service of our patients, but we are putting love in action.

Why is it so difficult to speak of love? Possibly because it might be viewed as inappropriate. It is not. Making the extra effort to reach out to others enriches our own lives.

I will appreciate the truly amazing work that I'm called to do and the caring that takes place. There is value in slowing down and being grateful.

Teamwork and the Restless
Attitude to Excel

There is a popular saying that "teamwork is the fuel that allows common people to attain uncommon results." "Common people" may not sound exciting, but they are. Uncommon results may not seem unusual. They are.

The construction of spectacular buildings, monuments or bridges is a physical reminder of the power of teamwork. No one ever built a bridge by himself. But, there are many examples of teamwork. Here are two.

A team in our hospital created a Centering Pregnancy program. The entire practice attended the initial training, even those not particularly excited about providing prenatal care a different way. In this program, every team member has a voice and volunteers their time to do the work required of the group. Not only has the Centering team successfully implemented a program that begins a new group every month, they have introduced Centering Pregnancy for Spanish speaking women and pregnant teens. The shared mission and values keep the entire team aligned, and the victories and challenges are shared by the entire practice. They are a remarkable example of a high functioning team.

Another example was the building and opening of a new medical center. What a team effort to accomplish such a massive project on time and on budget! They shared a common goal, vision, and dream, which created a feeling of camaraderie that fueled their accomplishments. Each team member pitched in to do whatever was needed. There were no questions about job titles, job descriptions, role clarity or asking, "who was responsible for doing this?" The power of such alignment and working in unison was evident in what they were able to accomplish.

Those working to construct a new hospital or clinic know the value of working as a team to achieve uncommon results. No one on those teams would think for a moment that they could do the job alone. The same is true for people working in any hospital, clinic, treatment center or physician practice. Within those walls, teams of individuals are providing extraordinary clinical care and service by combining their talents. No individual working alone, not even the most highly talented, can do what he or she does without the help of others. It takes a team that is united in purpose, plan and vision. It requires a surrendering of ego to the greater good of this common goal.

It is inspiring to think that this is possible, that by sharing a vision with others, together, we can achieve amazing results.

Am I clear about my team's or organization's vision and my role in it? What can I do to recommit to this vision?

Changing the Mood with Our Words

Our moods are shaped by many factors—external events—the weather, and our health—among other things. Children, especially, can change our mood in an instant. Just think of a child running excitedly into your arms. It can brighten your whole day in an instant. Our colleagues, too, can have a profound affect on our mood, particularly ones who sport a generally optimistic view of life. The happiest people on earth are the ones who are grateful. They see everything, including their own lives, as a gift.

Our own speech also influences how we feel. That is because the spoken word lingers and collects in our memory. Remember when a colleague or your boss complimented you on a particular assignment or task? The next time you approached a similar task or even a new one, you were likely filled with more confidence and enthusiasm. Similarly, after receiving a comment that was not offered in a helpful spirit, we could have felt burdened, resentful or even insecure about our abilities. The impact of one person's words influences how we feel as well as how we work.

Think of the power we have to change a person's mood when we genuinely compliment him or her on a job well done, encourage a colleague who is trying to develop fresh skills, or help someone who is taking on new responsibilities. Like so many seemingly ordinary and daily activities, we can view these words and actions as having a sacred quality about them. "Sacred" may seem like an unusual word to use to describe speech. Words are sacred because they change other people, ourselves, and our surroundings. As we speak, we create, perhaps co-create, the world around us. That is an unnerving responsibility. Taking time to reflect on the importance of our words is one more way to recognize our value as individuals, our influence on our colleagues, and the opportunity to be a healing presence to our patients.

Today, I will consciously use my words to create the world I want to work in. I will shape my mood and make a positive contribution by complimenting coworkers, acknowledging achievements and encouraging new efforts. I can make a difference with my words.

Valuing Volunteerism

In another section of this book, we mentioned "vocation-loving" individuals—that is, those who want to do what they actually have to do. Most of us divide what we want and what we must do into two buckets. One we call work, the other, leisure. Then, we set about trying to balance the two or make sure that time for one does not encroach on the other. Vocation-loving individuals do not split the two.

There is also volunteering. It's not work because you do not get paid. Yet, it's not leisure; it's hard work. People do it because they want to help. Many vocation-loving people have more energy left at the end of the day and volunteer their free time after work. They even bring their children with them in an effort to integrate their home life and work life.

Health care is filled with people who are imbued with a sense of giving. Many hospital personnel have a history of volunteering to work in developing countries.

The generosity of our physicians and employees, both current and retired, is one more indication that beneath the hustle and bustle of daily life, there lives a genuine yearning of the human spirit to be of help to others, selflessly.

I will look for ways to give back to my community, whether it is within miles of where I live or on the other side of the world.

Carrying Our Inner Lives to Work

All of us have lives apart from work. We bring that outside life to work each day. Here are two examples:

Some of our employees have family members serving in the armed services. One employee in the Facilities Department spoke of what it was like to have a son in Iraq. He spoke of the emotional strain of just listening to the morning news and hearing the words, "Three of our soldiers were killed earlier today...." The father always had to wait two weeks to find out if his son was among them. A man in this position carries a weight we can only imagine.

Another employee who worked on the third floor was entering the building when I met up with her right before the elevator. She was so excited that her eyes actually glistened. She was pregnant and was only a few days from delivery. Her enthusiasm was positively contagious. I stepped into the elevator; she did not. When the doors opened on the third floor, there she was!

"How did you get here?" I asked.
"The steps," she said.
"Why not the elevator?"
"Because I'm trying to take care of myself as well as my baby."

She managed to find little ways to get exercise and care for her pregnancy, even as she made her way to her office to begin her work day. She was creative in how she was able to care for herself and her unborn child, while at the same time doing her job.

These are some common examples of how our personal experiences color our work life. The emotional lines blur between home and work; between our inner and our outer lives. All of us have an inner sanctuary where we hold concerns. Simply recognizing the influence that these have on our work life and being open to the inner lives of our colleagues and patients, allows for a richer work experience and greater tolerance for all.

Today, I will respect my coworkers, patients and others with whom I come in contact. I will look for ways to care for myself and be sensitive to the inner lives of my coworkers.

$\mathcal{B}$y Caring for One Another
We Create a Culture of Care

Working in health care creates challenges. Those of us with patient contact walk through the doors of our work place and are immediately drawn into meeting the needs of people who are in a great deal of discomfort, pain, or who perhaps are dying. Those of us not involved directly in patient care have equally demanding responsibilities. Both types of work challenge us to be selfless.

Recently, there was a memorial service for one of our employees, a young woman who worked for many years at one of our hospitals. At least fifty employees were in attendance at the service, which was the second one held in her memory. The first was for her family; this one was for us. During the service, photographs flashed onto a screen behind the altar. Most were of her and friends (many of whom were employees) scaling mountains, canoeing, and enjoying one another. A friend remarked that even when she was dying of cancer, she was the life of the party and people seemed drawn to her. "Most days there were five or six people hanging around her home in the evening, sometimes as many as thirty people. She was extremely lively and welcoming. She exuded life."

Our colleague's death reminds us of how important we are to one another. We are a community. We need one another. We spend much time at work. Some of us work ten hours a day, many longer. Friendships are made. Often enough, we party or go out to eat with one another. There are even leagues where we bowl on Friday and Saturday evenings. Some ski, others bike together. In a manner of speaking the work place resembles a village in bygone days where it provided for almost all of the villagers' needs.

While our focus at work is always on our patients, we are also part of a larger community of colleagues where we care for one another, and where each person has a role to play in creating the climate. By taking a second look at the people in our work community and attempting to get to know them better, we not only enrich our lives, but we cultivate trust, which makes working together easier, especially when we're under pressure.

A culture of care isn't just for patients or just for colleagues. Caring for one another doesn't take away from our capacity to care for patients; in fact, it enhances it. While it may be difficult to prove, the more sensitive we are to one another, the better service we will provide for our patients.

I will contribute toward building a community of caring by expanding my focus to include my colleagues and their needs. I will take a moment to get to know someone a little better and I will reveal a little more about myself.

Avoidance

Scott Peck, the psychiatrist, opened his best seller, The Road Less Traveled with this first line, "Life is difficult." He then went on to describe how we try to avoid life's inevitable problems, and as a result, have a tendency to create even more trouble for ourselves. The book outlines how we can change that approach by delaying gratification and facing problems head-on, knowing that the payoff will come later by taking responsibility for one's life, by being dedicated to truth, and by cultivating the skill of balancing emotional reactions and the unavoidable highs and lows. The book artfully explores the importance of being flexible, learning how to give up parts of ourselves while still remaining true to our values. In his view, love fuels all of these efforts.

After twenty-five years, the book is still popular largely because most of us recognize our tendency to avoid painful difficulties. Yet we also want to learn how to respond in a more courageous and authentic way. In a nutshell, it takes courage and self-discipline to stand by our convictions.

I know the problems associated with staying in a job when I knew I should have moved on. I was working in a hospital system and reporting to an individual with whom I found it difficult to work. Maybe it was solely my issue, maybe hers. Likely both. In retrospect, I would say that we were mismatched as players who, unfortunately, were charged with trying to get the work done in an integrated, coordinated manner. Our conflicting styles made working in a close partnership challenging. While others affirmed my performance and wanted me to stay (including the CEO to whom we both reported), I recognized that I needed to leave. I did not—at least not right away. Why? It was a case of fear mixed with a touch of stubbornness.

Most of us have been in situations where we have had to make a decision whether to begin a difficult conversation or to avoid it. We sacrifice a lot when we avoid expressing our views. Avoidance diminishes pride in our work, eats away at our commitment to excellence and leaks out in interactions with coworkers and patients as pessimism and cynicism.

Excellence in clinical care and service requires that we have, at times, difficult conversations. Why? Because if we want there to be continuous improvement, we have to challenge the way things have always been done, accept new approaches, question the value of our pet projects, and even terminate a work relationship that is "easy" but not serving patients or supporting quality care efforts.

It would certainly be easier to coast through the workday, avoid making suggestions, and look the other way when we see an injustice or a mismanaged department. A few may say, "Better to plod along, stay in the crowd, and avoid lofty aspirations. Settle for being average." Yet, this is not the path to greatness. Avoiding difficulties actually increases rather than resolves problems.

If we want to create an organization that is not only committed to excellence but is aligned with our personal and professional values, we have to support a climate that encourages others to initiate difficult conversations. Risky conversations can produce amazing results if we engage in them with the purest of intention honestly and with the intention of improving the quality of patient care. Questioning takes courage and is the boldest of beginnings.

I will reflect on the courage and self-discipline I need to speak out and express my needs and opinions. I will initiate a difficult conversation, if necessary, and I will live a life of integrity.

Attitudes about Money Shape How We Treat Others

Money is a problem. Our attitude toward money, which is often a charged topic, reveals many insights about ourselves. The problem is that we do not always talk about it in an honest and open way. Just because we don't discuss it does not mean that it does not influence our dealings with others.

Ironically, while we may not discuss money at work, the culture around us seems preoccupied with it. TV programs are devoted to tracking financial markets. Financial advice is offered 24 hours a day on the Money channel. Game shows seemingly give away millions much to our delight. Turn on the TV after midnight and you'll preview one get-rich-quick scheme after another, all playing on people's hopes of discovering instant riches.

You do not have to be in a health care organization very long to know that it and the financial world are tightly interconnected. Despite our highest intention to be solely on a mission of healing, many decisions are financially driven.

On the other hand, talking directly about money is uncomfortable, even if it is at the top of our worry list. Few of us reveal our salaries to our colleagues. Often, we secretly believe that this dollar amount says something important about our worth as individuals. It reflects our value in the eyes of our employer. Telling others what we make will not only expose some hidden truth about our worth but may stir up comparisons, competition and conflict among our colleagues.

The dollar amount in our paycheck also holds great sway over how we view ourselves. High salaries tend to enhance our self-worth. Being under-employed diminishes how we feel about ourselves and our abilities.

Honest conversations about money are hard to come by even in the privacy of our home life. Parents find it difficult to talk about their savings to their adult children for fear that either they will think of them as less successful, or that they'll pressure them to share their assets. Not surprisingly, every marriage counselor is trained to look for the hidden and unacknowledged role that money plays in troubled relationships because how it is spent, saved, and discussed (or not) speaks volumes about the degree of honesty, the power-balance and the values within the relationship. Despite the undergrounding of financial matters, the values and power dynamics surrounding money—how it is spent or saved—wield strong influence over marriages.

Walk down the street and notice the homeless on the sidewalk. It will remind you of the role that money plays in life. We may think, "There but for the grace of God go I," or we may wonder what they have done to end up in this predicament. When our eyes meet, we handle our unease by turning away.

You may ask, "So what if I harbor these feelings about money? What does that have to do with working in a hospital and dealing with patients?" As health care professionals, we come in contact with the full spectrum of society, from the very rich to the very poor, and regardless of their financial status, we are committed to improving their health. Knowing that our deeply held beliefs about money—whether we admit to them or not—influence our actions, we are obligated to take a more pensive look at how our beliefs impact the way we treat our patients and their families.

As professionals, we serve our communities very well, often exceptionally so. Yet, a number of recently published studies indicate that the caregiver's perception of a patient's financial resources may significantly lower the quality of care. If we don't take the time and have the courage to uncover these truths about our attitudes, they will continue to direct our actions, maybe in ways that conflict with our equally strongly-held values of providing exceptional and fair and safe treatment to all, regardless of the person's financial standing. Whatever the truth may be for you, this moment, like every moment, is a good time to look inward.

Do I change my level of care depending on my perception of a patient's economic situation? Every individual has dignity; each life is sacred.

Memorial Day: Learning from Those Who've Gone Before Us

Memorial Day isn't only about White Sales at Macy's or barbecues in the backyard. It is an opportunity to commemorate the people who have died in service to our country. Those who serve in the armed services never serve alone. They are always someone's child, husband, wife, relative, buddy, or colleague. When one person goes off to serve his country, he leaves behind a whole circle of people who miss his presence and worry about him. "No man is an island" is an oft-used phrase, and it is true.

All of our lives are built on the lives of those who have gone before us. Soldiers sacrifice theirs so that we can keep ours. We have what we have because of them. A wordless prayer of gratitude will not lessen the tragedy of their loss, but it is surely a fitting response.

We can turn this day of memory into an opportunity for bettering this world by listening to those who have died. To hear them speak, all we have to do is be quiet for a moment or two. What do you think a young man of twenty-two who was blown up by an IED would say to his grieving mother? What would the father who died on foreign soil say to his son who will now grow up without him? While we often think of these soldiers as without names, they are not. They are our teachers and they are continually reminding us of what is important in life.

None of us knows the words that our loved ones would speak. Likely, they would counsel us to live deliberately and without regret.

Today, I will be grateful for those soldiers who've sacrificed their lives. I will honor their lives by carrying on in their memory.

The Stillness of Being a Healing Presence

To define the word presence is difficult. People will say, "Of course I'm present. I know I'm here. What else is there?" But to be truly present is to be attentive to them, not to ourselves. That is very difficult to do.

What does it mean to be a healing presence? It means that we are attentive in a manner whereby the other person feels healed. It involves a profound act of sharing. When someone is ill or dying, being a healing presence is invaluable.

To be a healing presence, we must be genuinely present to the other person in need. By opening up our heart and spirit to the other, the suffering one will feel connected. This is a gift to be cherished.

Often, particularly when people are ill, they can feel terribly alone. As author Anne Morrow Lindberg said, there is not a greater gift than when "two solitudes touch." That is another way to describe what it means to be a healing presence.

We cannot be a healing presence while we are self-absorbed. Being pre-occupied by anything other than the person to whom we minister hinders our presence. Rambling thoughts take us away from bringing ourselves into the present moment. Surprisingly, we are never more in touch with ourselves than when we are present to the other.

We can learn how to be a healing presence to others. Take time to be quiet. Work at becoming reflective. Take a few minutes to sit with what you are feeling.

Being a healing presence is more than sharing feelings or advice. It is often experienced by others as peacefulness, quiet, and stillness. Nothing lessens a patient's fears more than when we share this precious gift. Human companionship lessens pain and calms anxieties. We benefit as well.

Today, I will try something new. I will take a few deep breaths before entering a patient's room or begin a meeting. I will see how my life is enriched when I open myself to be present to another.

$\mathcal{P}$urposeful Reflection:
Do You Truly Value Time?

Time is a precious commodity, and perhaps our most prized possession. Life is a gift. When we talk about time, it is easy to dismiss the deeper meaning of these seemingly trite, simple expressions. Slow down and examine the truth behind it.

The reality is that our lives are time-bound—we have only so many moments. Recognizing time as a precious commodity is an invitation to use it wisely.

When we think of life's hours as limited and precious, it lets us examine what we value. Each of us knows how we need to use the time. The question is, do we have the courage to act on what we know?

Reflecting purposefully on the notion of time is one more invitation to live honestly, to use our time well, to love genuinely, and to die having devoted ourselves to life-enabling and valued activities.

Whatever responsibilities we have, whether at a bedside, in an operating room, or a windowless office, whether repairing what is broken, cleaning what is soiled, or carefully bandaging what is tender, all of us are valued and all of our jobs are important.

Today, I will purposefully reflect on how I use my time. I will be courageous in my use of time. I will use it to love genuinely and serve with purpose. I will be aware of the precious gift of time that I've been given and I will use it with a sense of purpose.

Bringing Anticipation, Re-Dedication and Celebration to Our Work

Christmas is the season of anticipation. Christian churches celebrate what is called Advent, a time of anticipation leading up to the birth of Jesus. Believing that God took on human flesh, is another way that Christians express their belief in the sacredness of the world.

It is also a season of remembering and spiritual rededication for the Jewish community. As they celebrate Hannukah, they recall the events that led up to the rededication of the Temple of Jerusalem. The ritual of lighting a candle each day for eight days, represents a time in ancient history when a Jewish tribe, the Maccabees, fought for the freedom to worship according to their beliefs. At the end of the fighting all they could find in their destroyed temple was enough oil to light a lamp for a day. Miraculously, the oil kept the lamp lit for eight days. This story inspires Jews to appreciate their religious freedom to rededicate themselves to their religion.

This season of religious events bring us back to our spiritual roots. If we slow down, we can feel the sacredness of the season. In the midst of daily work life, whatever our faith tradition, we can let this hallowed time influence our work with the qualities of anticipation, re-dedication and celebration that these holidays represent.

I will seize this day to revitalize my work with the anticipation, re-dedication and celebration taught by the people of the past. I can learn and benefit from many traditions.

Learning from Failure

Recently, I was with a person who was directly involved in a situation that nearly resulted in serious harm to a patient. She felt incredibly responsible and had the strength of character to speak openly of how she unknowingly contributed to the patient's injury. While others admired her for her ability to speak honestly, she nevertheless felt terrible. In fact, she felt like a failure.

Most of the time, we think of failure as something bad. On the contrary, it is a time for learning. Times of success are periods for resting. When we're successful, there are fewer opportunity to challenge our thinking, make mistakes and learn. Success is enjoyable; failure is painful. We need both to grow.

Think of the story of Adam and Eve. Adam and Eve walked blissfully in the Garden of Good and Evil. Life was lovely and free from stress. They were unaware that they were naked. What happened when they did something wrong? When they failed? They became aware that they were naked. They became conscious. Failure is the path to awareness. It is through failure and awareness that we grow.

While failure is uncomfortable and something none of us welcomes, it is nevertheless a graced moment. Like it or not, failure is the soil from which learning rises.

Today, I'll take a moment to reflect on times when I've failed. When situations arise where I fall short, I will not berate myself but learn from them.

Being Sensitive to the Hidden Lives of Others

Before one particular physicians' meeting began, I heard a conversation among a few physicians. One said she was a 5-year cancer survivor and passionately expressed her gratitude that she was alive. Then she added, "I never really thought about God until this happened to me." Those who listened seemed not to know how to respond when she mentioned God, and so the conversation ended.

All of us struggle with how to respond to others when they bring up difficult topics. This is particularly true when we have strong feelings and opinions associated with the topic of conversation. Often, we hesitate to address certain topics, particularly our experience of God. It is a gift when the level of trust within an organization is developed to such a degree that we can risk exposing our beliefs and experiences.

The small group that heard the cancer-survivor speak appeared to find it difficult to respond to the physician. I suspect she felt exposed as a result of their inability to respond. If that is true, it's unfortunate for everyone involved. All of us have corners of our lives appropriately hidden from the prying eyes of others. As uncomfortable as it may be, it is not helpful to keep our experience of God permanently locked away.

Keeping alive a sensitivity to the hidden side of life—as unsettling as it is— helps us respond to others with genuine care. All of us need and deserve that sensitivity.

Life is richer when connections with people deepen.

When Flowers and Praise Aren't Enough

Clearly, anyone who is ill knows the value of a caring nurse or top-notch physician. Most patients also appreciate the unseen professionals who staff our hospitals and offices. While many patients might not think of them right away, they certainly value the contribution of behind-the-scenes employees who work in business services and as office assistants supporting those who offer direct care to patients.

If all of this is true, and patients really are appreciative of all we do, why don't we feel it? It is not as if they don't acknowledge us in touching ways. We often receive notes after they are discharged; loved ones will thank us for taking such good care of their grandmother, or sister or husband. Often, we don't take it in, or we need to hear it from our supervisor or manager for it to carry real weight.

The perspective of the novelist Anna Quindlen is helpful. When speaking to the graduates of a leading university, she said, "There are thousands of people doing what you want to do for a living. But you will be the only person alive who has sole custody of your life, your particular life, your entire life. I have learned that [life] is not a dress rehearsal. Learn to be happy. Think of life as a terminal illness because if you do, you will live it with joy and passion, as it ought to be lived." What she is saying is that feeling valued starts with us! It's nice to get the flowers and the recognition, but if our happiness and sense of satisfaction from our work relies on these outward displays, surely we will be disappointed.

We are on a journey to be the best that we can be. We want to be the best for the sake of our patients, not for self-adulation. By taking control of my work and being the best at what I do, I will know that my contribution is valuable and I will feel valued. I will look for ways to acknowledge the value of others' contributions.

Expressing Our Uniqueness

Yesterday, by chance, while waiting in line for coffee, I met one of our employees who was talking with a nurse from a neighboring hospital about her own three children. Clearly, she loved being a mom. "I think I'm a natural at it. I wouldn't trade it for the world." Then she said something that startled me. "This morning I realized that no one else can take my place. This is what I was born to do!"

She was not implying that no one else in the world was a good mother. She was saying that she was pulled to become a mother and she brings something unique to the job. In today's world, seldom do we hear people speak of themselves in terms of being "called" to do anything; this presumes that someone or some thing is beckoning and actively playing a role in the work we do. Many of us act at times, as if we are independent players, acting without the pull of an inner calling.

Martin Luther King Jr. lived with a sense that he was "called" and that something was being asked of him. John Henry Newman, a nineteenth century Englishman who, at mid-life, converted to Catholicism and was later made a cardinal, struggled in much the same way before he was able to pen his recognition that, "God created me to do some definite service; he has committed some work to me which he has not committed to another." This was the same sentiment expressed by the mother in the coffee shop.

Victor Frankl was the physician-writer who reminded us that no job, however esteemed by others, provides meaningful employment. A job simply provides an opportunity for an individual to discover his or her uniqueness. While there are many moms in this world, the coffee shop mom knew that she was a unique and irreplaceable person especially to her own children. That insight is priceless.

Many of us may not feel particularly valued. In fact, we may and believe that we are easily replaceable. Every one of us, whether at the bedside of patients or supporting those who are, is irreplaceable. Our challenge is to awaken to our unique talents and provide opportunities to express them.

I am a unique collection of talents, experiences and character. Their expression is my unique contribution.

Taking the Time to Be Attentive

Yesterday, I was alone on an elevator with two physicians. One asked, "Any New Year's resolutions?" "Actually, yes," said the other, "I really want to try to be more present to people, not only the patients, but even my family." Clearly the physicians were friends, but I was amazed that they spoke with such intimacy on an elevator. I did not know either of them.

As one of the physicians got off the elevator but before the door closed, he quipped, "I wish I had your faith in being able to change yourself. I can't remember the last time I made a New Year's resolution."

When the doors closed, I had a flashback to an event where my own inability to be attentive and present had an incalculable cost. I was a practicing psychologist in a highly specialized psychiatric hospital. With the support of others on her treatment team, I had approved a patient's request for a two-day home visit during the holidays. While at home, she purchased a bottle of an over-the-counter medication. When she returned to the hospital, she combined her prescribed medications with what she bought, overdosed, and died.

Why did that memory pop into my mind after the conversation between the two physicians on the elevator? Perhaps because the physician spoke of her desire to be more attentive to others. I have always wondered if I was as present to that patient as I needed to be. If I had not missed her intense pain and hidden need, could her life have been different? And then, there's the question of our ability to change. I had to ask myself, "Have I become more attentive to others' needs since then?"

Within health care, our mission is to foster the health and healing of our patients. It is easy to forget that before we can bring a healing presence to others, we first have to slow down to be present. To work with those who genuinely try to be present to one another is an immense gift. We benefit as employees and most importantly, our patients benefit.

Today, I will try to be present to my patients, coworkers, friends and family. I will demonstrate this in my words and actions. I will also look for ways to encourage my coworkers to have the composure and state of mind to be present. This is the greatest gift I can give them and myself.

Creating a Positive Work Climate

A few months ago, I attended a dinner honoring employees and physicians who had a long history of service. Everyone was seated and the invocation was about to begin when a few hungry guests began eating prematurely. Someone remarked lightly, "Hey, you can't eat. Don't you know the food hasn't been blessed yet?" One of the people who had dug into her plate, did not pick up on the humor. In all seriousness she said, "I know, but I don't want others who have already started eating to feel uncomfortable."

It was a small thing, yet it showed a remarkable sensitivity. The woman was so aware of the feelings of others that even though, on her own, she would have waited to take her first bite, for the sake of others she discarded convention to put them at ease.

This is a helpful quality for those of us who work with patients. When people are hospitalized, they are sensitive to the atmosphere of the hospital. They pick up on it when two nurses don't like each other, or when one doctor shows disrespect. Ill will never helps the healing process.

Every time we answer a phone, glance at someone passing us in the hallway or ask for help, the occasion is there to bring a feeling of goodwill to the work space. It isn't just those who may be in supervisor or managerial positions who affect others. Accountants, office assistants, clerks, electricians, nutritionists, nurses and purchasing agents have an impact on the climate of the work place. The fellow who mops the floor can make a big difference with a smile or a kind word to staff and patients.

Every act creates the world. The challenge is to recognize that daily life, itself, is a sacred act. We are players on a hallowed stage, writing our own lines as we perform.

I will make a conscious effort to create a more positive work place. I will be an influence for good, creating the kind of place where I want to spend my workday.

$\mathcal{T}$*he Need for Diversity*

On Martin Luther King Jr. Day, we remember a charismatic leader, a man who awakened hope for so many, and who taught many more of us to recognize the injustice of our ways. His famous "I Have a Dream" speech was filled with hope and vision: "I have a dream ... that one day little black boys and black girls will be able to join hands with little white boys and white girls as sisters and brothers."

When we work in a hospital, we are in the quintessential melting pot. No matter where you live in the country, you are working with people from many races and all socio-economic levels. We need to acknowledge the differences, yes, but more importantly, recognize what we have in common as human beings.

This is a particularly special holiday for people of color because King was in the forefront of a movement to demand equality for all Americans. They are rightfully proud of their heritage and, each of them is a gift to our organization because they bring their unique perspective to the work place.

Diversity is more than a gift; it is a necessity. Why? In part, because our patients are diverse and we need to be able to reflect their world back to them. When this mirroring is in place, it creates an immediate sense of trust and understanding. If we are driven to excellence, and we are, how can we serve patients well without being an equally diverse staff? We cannot.

In Starbucks this afternoon, a particularly obnoxious patron asked another, "Why should Black people have a special holiday?" Clearly, he did not understand that Monday is not a holiday for a few, but for all of us. It is the day we again remember what one man taught us, and what is so easily forgotten: "That all men are created equal, that they are endowed by their Creator with certain unalienable rights, that among these are Life, Liberty and the pursuit of Happiness."

Today, I will look at others with a renewed sensitivity and appreciation. By honoring the diversity and rights of my colleagues and patients, everyone benefits, including me.

Bringing Mind, Body and Spirit to Our Work

Last evening, PBS aired a special on the life of Thomas Jefferson. Toward the end of the program, the narrator read from the President's diary, where he wrote that his personal challenge was to "integrate mind, heart and hand."

If someone as important as the third President of a fledgling nation declares this as his biggest challenge—not balancing the budget, not mediating between two political parties, not running the country—then it must be worth considering. We would expect to read such lyrical words in the works of philosophers or poets, not from a politician. Hospital work, too, is practical and hands-on, yet in order to raise our performance to the level of the excellence we desire, we must engage our minds, and hearts as well as our hands, to the daily tasks we encounter.

We all know how it feels to work from our intellect and without our heart. People who operate this way might become technically proficient but they're hardly personable. Those we touch can feel the difference.

And from within ourselves, we know what it feels like when our bodies are at work yet our minds are elsewhere; we tend to feel detached. A detached workforce is not the soil from which genuine care and excellence in care rise.

On the other hand, we all know people whose hearts are in the right place, but they are not focused or grounded. They tend to be ineffective. A hospital cannot serve its patients without a staff that can carry out its practical duties.

As Jefferson wrote, we need to integrate heart, mind and hand together. The challenge is to create the kind of work place where this is possible. We have to ask ourselves, "Is anything getting in the way?" Some say new policies and procedures are needed. Others point a finger at senior management or at another department. We need to look at ourselves first to discover what is missing. As Jefferson knew so well, change begins with the individual. It begins at this moment, in this place, with this person, doing this task.

Today, I will improve the quality of my work by integrating my knowledge, my heart and my hands into all that I do. I am responsible for my actions and the work environment I help create.

Using Tragedy and Illness to Be Mindful of Life and Work

Each year we remember and perhaps re-live the emotions we felt on September 11, 2001. Our sense of national invulnerability was exposed and we had to rethink our views of the world and our place in it. The catastrophe ruptured our sense of trust and awakened the suspicious side of our nature, making us hyper-vigilant towards people from other cultures.

How we respond to tragedy reveals how we approach life-altering events and the fear that accompanies them. Some people panicked after 9-11 and wanted heads to roll. They were hardened by the visions of horror. For others, the memory of that day provided an opportunity to reflect on its meaning—that you never know when death will strike. It could be a sunny Tuesday morning. Their response is to live each day as if it were their last. Still others were simply stunned and didn't know what their response to this disaster should be. All they could do was sit in silence.

Illness as well as tragedy can help us think about life in fresh ways if we let it. For example, when a woman came into the business office to ask about her bill, she was living with the thought that she may never see another Thanksgiving. Instead of dispassionately shoving a fistful of papers at her to sign, the clerk took the time to ask her if there was anything he could do to help. He sat her down and simply acknowledged how hard this might be. "I'm sorry I have to ask you to sign these at a time like this." Just that tiny acknowledgement made it easier for her to walk out of the hospital. The clerk did not just see his job as getting the papers signed. He broadened his view of his job to include reaching out to a frightened woman.

We can all transform the impact of 9-11 by letting it soften us instead of harden us. We can open to the deeper human connection we are capable of having with each other.

Today, I will use tragedy to transform how I live my day. By changing my attitude, I will honor the lives of those changed on September 11 and the lives of others who have been altered by tragedy.

Valuing Vacation

August is vacation time for many. Since health care is a 365-day commitment, many employees are in the midst of negotiating time to be away. There is always a give-and-take involved in these negotiations simply because of the need to cover for one another.

Most people now think of vacations as a means of escape. Ford Motor Company actually named their mini SUV "Escape"; billboards carry a photo of the car and seven words: "Escape," "Your Boss," "Your Job," "Your World." As catchy as that advertisement is, few of us in health care take vacations solely to escape our boss, job or world.

Our attitude is closer to the Greeks. In ancient times, travel was a way to gain wisdom. Cities would send ambassadors to faraway places to learn from others. Passage was so slow that the village people often waited for years to hear what the traveler had learned. Nowadays, going away to another land is not simply an attempt to break free from what binds us, but a genuine desire to learn.

Vacations serve a far more important function than merely offering us an opportunity to relax. They have a way of giving us a perspective on what is important in life and they tend to strengthen our commitment to patients.

How we are present to ourselves and to the world—even on vacation—determines the quality of the time away and the measure of refreshment we feel when we return.

Some health care professionals are so devoted to their patients and to their work that they don't take all of their vacation time. That is unfortunate. Everyone, even the most dedicated, need time away.

Everyone needs a change of scenery, and I will be doing my colleagues, my family and myself a favor by taking time off!

Our Work Matters:
It's All in Your Perspective

When hospitals, clinics, or physician offices are being constructed or opened, a new world is being created. An observer may think it is simply another construction project or business venture. It is, but there is another way of thinking about it. A building is more than just a building. A shift in perspective will illuminate that moments in every day life hold more meaning than we realize.

Architects and caregivers have one thing in common: they both use the materials around them to build something new. If poets, philosophers, theologians or saints were commenting, they would refer to our activity as co-creating an ever-changing world. No caregiver ever does anything alone. Everything we accomplish is a collaborative effort, borrowing from the strengths of each person.

Another thing we share with builders and architects is that our work also goes far beyond our own lifetime. Many of the men who build roads, bridges and skyscrapers have died, yet their legacy is left for others to enjoy. Similarly, the pioneers who invented new drug regiments, innovative prosthetic devices, and revolutionary medical procedures which are now considered routine, have passed on, but their legacy of ideas, hard work and dedication live on in us and in the patients fortunate to receive the benefits of their creativity, energy and talent. And, if we think through the domino effect of our work, the life we save or extend impacts families almost beyond comprehension. How a child remembers her dad, if a grandchild ever gets to enjoy experiences with a grandmother, whether a son ever takes a walk with his mother again—all of these stories and lives become a part of our legacy and the work that we do.

By taking a bigger view of our work, we can see that everything we do collectively matters greatly. Recognizing the sacredness of what we are about has a way of changing how we think of our jobs.

I will stand back and look at my work from a larger perspective. I will see how my work impacts the world around me, now and in the future.

$\mathcal{T}$ruly Listening

At the start of a regularly scheduled meeting, we took a few minutes to check in with each other before tackling the work at hand. The practice of taking this time is part of the hospital's culture. A nurse spoke up, "I'm not satisfied with the way we're communicating with each other. People are so busy putting out fires, they can't slow down enough to listen carefully to their colleagues—whether to fill orders or to share a personal moment."

The Director of Communications was asked her ideas about how to create this. Given her highly developed interpersonal skills and professional training, I expected her to offer tips to help us slow down the pace of our lives. Instead, she talked about her daughter. "One day when I was at home and having what I thought was a significant conversation with my daughter, she stopped and said, 'Mom, listen to me.' I said that I was. 'No Mom,' she said, 'listen to me with your face.'"

Her daughter needed to see and feel that she had her mother's full attention or it wasn't a real conversation. This girl has something to teach all of us. While we may have a difficult time trying to describe what it means to "listen with your face," I think we can sense what it means. The need to be heard and seen is genuine. Because our patients are so vulnerable, they may not have the freedom that children do to honestly tell us that they need us to "listen with our faces." An integral part of healing is the quality of human contact a patient experiences during the time they are with us.

Today, I will make a conscious to listen to those who are in pain and vulnerable. I may be the right person to help them today.

Expressing Empathy

Every day thousands of nurses, physicians, and clinical personnel are engaged at the bedside of patients. Hundreds more care for patients in offices and clinics. For every clinician directly involved with patient care, there are three support personnel who seldom have direct contact with patients. For people in both groups, it is easy to forget what it is like to be a patient. The essayist Anna Quindlen holds this perspective when she speaks of being a teenager and experiencing her mother's death from ovarian cancer. Her life changed forever.

"One day you [are] walking around worrying about whether you [have] anything to wear to a party, and reminding yourself to buy kitty litter or toilet paper. And then you [are] in the shower lathering up, or you [are] lying on a doctor's table, or the phone rings. And your world suddenly divides, as my world did many years ago. It divides into 'before' and 'after.'"

Once you know your days are limited, it is not easy to take life for granted again.

Most of us have had experiences where our lives seem to be rolling along and our solitary focus is on crossing off the classic errands from our list. We are rushing from one store to the next wondering how we're going to get it all done, when out of the blue, news of a friend's death or a family member's scary diagnosis instantly suspends our life. Nothing before that matters and the future seems suddenly scary and uncertain. Every patient can tell you about such a moment, when they were shaken with the knowledge of their mortality. Some day, we too will be patients, and as vulnerable as those we currently serve.

Reflecting on these ideas can help us in our work. When we send out bills, answer phones, place orders for medical equipment, maintain schedules for office personnel, assure clean and comfortable rooms for patients, launder bed linens, or count pills for a prescription, we are caring for others at particularly vulnerable times in their lives. Doing it with kindness, warmth, and humor—whoever they may be and however they might look—is immensely important. It's tragic to care for others without empathy and compassion. Remembering how it feels to be vulnerable makes it easier to serve others with the compassion they deserve.

Today, I will think back on a time when I was vulnerable. What was most comforting for me? Who was the most healing person for me at that time?

Making Eye Contact

On the way to work, while sitting at a stoplight, I noticed, but looked away from, a young homeless man standing on the corner with the sign that read, "Anything will help." As I fiddled with the radio, I looked up again. Now, he was at the side of my car, no more than a foot from my window. Our eyes met. Usually, I do not give to people standing on street corners, but this time there was something about his eyes and face that changed my attitude. They called for a response, and I gave him some money.

Throughout the day, I remembered that man's eyes. I also had flashbacks of times when I have avoided others' eyes. I particularly remember my decades-long practice of sitting in nursing stations with my head down while charting. I consciously wanted to avoid eye contact so I could finish my work, afraid that if our eyes met, I'd be asked to take care of someone's needs.

Do I mention these experiences to showcase my inadequacies? No. Am I just trying to encourage others to give money to people on street corners? No. I want to show what I think happens all the time: that when eyes meet, individuals cannot ignore each other anymore.

We know that words are important for communicating, but we forget that eye contact does the same. Do you think that the quality of clinical care is enhanced when we look at our patients and one another?

We are seriously engaged in the process of developing an organization that is intent on providing our patients the highest possible level of clinical care and service. Everyone, including the homeless, can teach us how to do that.

Improving the quality of care can come in small, quiet changes, like meeting the eyes of patients and coworkers when all I really want to do is avoid them. I will take the risk and meet the eyes of my coworkers and my patients today.

Holding to Our Caring Convictions During Tight Financial Times

It's not uncommon for messages to come down from senior management announcing a new phase of belt tightening. Anyone who has worked in our field for any length of time has experienced the constant balancing act that health care organizations face in treating the uninsured or underinsured in our community while still coming up with the financial resources to pay for staff, maintenance of equipment, growth, as well as the operational costs associated with running a top-notch facility.

Unfortunately, when we have to function during a time of financial constraint, we operate with an attitude of scarcity—mixed with a little fear and anxiety associated with the loss of jobs. Employees who are challenged to do the same job with even fewer resources than they have now, are placed in an uncomfortable situation.

When these times arise, working harder is not an option because we're already tapped out. The mere suggestion that we work harder is a turn-off and increases stress.

We can better serve ourselves and our patients if we can resist this bunker mentality and instead, look for ways to work differently. Continuing a tradition of caring does not always mean using up a lot of money. There are ways to continue to care for our patients even during a period of tight budgets. As important as money is, all of the resources in the world will not guarantee quality care.

All of us have known colleagues who have reached into their own pockets or gone beyond their job description to help others in need. Here's an example of how one of our own showed compassion, generosity and innovative thinking toward one of his patients. One morning, we were discharging a homeless man from the hospital. He had no shoes. A nurse on the floor who was arranging for the patient's discharge took off his own new Nikes and gave them to the patient. "I've got another pair in my locker." We only found out later that not only did this nurse literally take the shoes off his own feet to give to this homeless man, but he did so knowing that he would be sacrificing his new pair for the older, worn out shoes in his locker.

This nurse's behavior is typical. Every day of the year in different ways, employees and physicians go out of their way for patients, usually unnoticed.

The behavior of the nurse giving away his shoes is one more hint that we can find an opportunity to genuinely care at any moment in any place within any organization. What we need is simply an appreciation of others and a generous spirit. As St. Francis of Assisi reminds us, "It is in giving that we receive."

I will do my part to spend my organization's money and resources wisely. I will also look for ways to work differently, smartly and with awareness. I will find unique ways to give.

The Saints Among Us

We tend to think of people who are a source of inspiration as saintly. The Albert Schweitzer's, the Florence Nightingale's, and the Mother Theresa's of this world hold our deeply held values and they model the best of what it means to be human.

Being sainted by popular acclaim, by church proclamation, or because one is part of a nation's history, is an extraordinary achievement that happens to very few people. However, the world is filled with individuals whose lives are inspirational, even though they're not written up in the newspaper. All we have to do is to take a second look at one another to find someone to uplift us.

Even the most ordinary life is full of hardship. No one is immune to bad luck, setbacks, heartache, illness and tragedy. Sometimes just to stay afloat, function and be a decent human being can take a super-human effort. Watch a duck serenely gliding across a pond seemingly without effort. If you look beneath the surface, you see its little webbed feet paddling furiously. It takes a lot of effort to make it look serene.

Once we manage to acknowledge the struggles that we have, we can recognize this achievement in others. From there, it is only a short step to appreciating the value, dignity, and even saintliness of people everywhere who are struggling the same way we are.

This might seem idealistic but actually looking beneath the surface has practical value. It helps us develop tolerance and empathy, become a better team player, and it keeps us from feeling alone with our personal suffering. Once we have cultivated this awareness of the universality of suffering, our shift in perspective lingers.

I will acknowledge my own triumphs and attempts to overcome struggle. I will also acknowledge the saintliness of my coworkers and patients as I observe them overcome their struggles.

Bringing Our Whole Self to the Work Place

In today's work place, we have to be sensitive to others' faiths and beliefs; we need to respect, not offend them. Many people believe that the only way to avoid offense is to keep their religious beliefs and values to themselves. There seems to be a sense that it's dangerous, especially at work, to express highly personal ideas that might be misinterpreted. As the contemporary poet, David Whyte, has written, it is little wonder that we feel we must leave part of ourselves at home when we come to work.

An example of this reluctance occurred during lunch one day. A nurse mentioned being uncomfortable speaking about her faith because she might seem insensitive to others at the table. She must have done a good job keeping her beliefs a secret because the person across from her said, "We've worked together for five years and I never knew you were Jewish." Then the office assistant at the far end of the table told all of us, for the first time, that she was a Latter Day Saint. "But," she added, "I keep it to myself." All it took was one person revealing her private truth for the truth of others to come spilling out. And guess what? Nothing catastrophic happened.

We do not want to create a work place where we bring only the functional side of ourselves to work. We want to foster a work culture that supports being whole and complete in every aspect of life. That means creating an environment where people aren't afraid to be visible, to discuss all facets of themselves.

It is true that it is safer to keep our most cherished spiritual beliefs to ourselves and remain quiet to avoid offending others. But, there's another way to respect others, which is to trust that sharing our beliefs will bring us closer together, not separate us. In our conversations, we can consciously approach others with an inquiring attitude, a readiness to discuss, and a desire to learn. When we do, respect takes on a whole new meaning.

I will look for ways to express myself authentically and encourage a respectful environment for others to do the same.

$\mathcal{I}t$ Takes a Team to Reduce Medical Errors

When tragic accidents happen—be they unforeseen medical errors, aviation accidents or gigantic industrial fires—scientists, researchers and administrators learn a lot from analyzing their root causes. They've found that seldom, if ever, is a single individual at fault.

There is always a "we" that leads to the problem and the problem usually points to a process that needs to be changed. When we are investigating how to reduce medical errors, we must think in terms of "we" by looking at the entire work place—people and processes—and see how weak links in communication among team members or a gap in checks and balances may be compromising the safety of our patients.

Sharing a common goal, like reducing medical errors or promoting patient safety, is part of a team's responsibility. And yet, a strong team is made up of committed individuals who effectively communicate with one another and contribute their unique strengths and talents toward a common team goal. Our responsibilities as members of a team are to speak up when we see broken processes that are jeopardizing patient safety. Without conscientious, vigilant individual members, the team as a whole fails. In health care, failure is tragic. A team is only as good as the individuals in it and their ability to work well together.

You may ask, "I'm only one member of a larger team. How can I make a difference?" For change to happen at a team level, and ultimately at an organizational level, it must begin with us, as individual members. We can start by creating a work culture that gives all of us the freedom to speak out about changes that need to be made. You and I play a critical part in creating a climate of safety within the work place. When a colleague feels that it is not safe to speak up, we have all participated in creating this climate. Each of us also has a role to play in changing it. If you doubt the influence of single individuals, recall how teams change when a member leaves or another joins.

By working together, we can create a work place that supports individuals and teams in their efforts to improve how care is delivered and work is done. This allows us to build a healing environment. This is not an unreasonable ideal; it is an obligation.

I will be part of the solution and look for ways to reduce medical errors. I will start by supporting an environment that rewards honesty and freedom to speak one's mind.

Two Holidays

In the spring, there are a number of religious holidays—for example, Purim for Jews and Easter for Christians. The feast of Purim is one of the most joyous for the Jewish people. It commemorates the time when Esther, the most favored and stunning woman in the king's harem, interceded with him to save her countrymen from being massacred. What the King did not know was that the woman he loved was a Jew. Her disguise saved her and her people. To this day, Jewish people sometimes don masks in carnival-like fashion to playfully reenact the memory of escaping death. The Jewish people have an enduring trust that G-d is protective and operates in largely unrecognized ways.

Easter is also a time of rejoicing within the Christian traditions, which vary according to their differing understandings of the resurrection of Jesus. However, Christians are united in their belief that the life of Jesus is risen. I met a patient dying of complications from cancer. "I love Easter," he said in a labored, quiet way, "All of my life I've recognized that there is something on the other side of disappointment and failure. I feel the same about death. Jesus died and rose. That has happened to me in little ways all through life. I feel the same as I lie here. I think that people who talk as if tough times are the end of everything haven't really lived." The spirit of Easter is something he carried with him throughout his life.

We are people with exceedingly different world views, yet one in our humanity. Let's help one another find time to remember the importance and magnitude of what we are about: nothing less than a special type of love for those entrusted to our care.

I will take the time to learn from traditions outside of my own. I will look for the common thread of humanity that binds us together.

Practicing the Art and Science of Medicine

The science of medicine changes constantly. We can be grateful that we live today, not yesterday. Only a hundred years ago, if you had tuberculosis you would likely die within a few years. The same if you had cardiac failure. Before penicillin, thousands died from infections and diseases that today are merely inconveniences. Our children will be blessed to live in tomorrow's world.

However radically the science of medicine changes from decade to decade, the art of practicing medicine has not. Two thousand years ago, a patient needed his physician's healing presence just as much as he does today. Many cultures and traditions have known for centuries the healing qualities that come from an understanding heart and a caring hand. With today's machines and new technologies, this side of medical care is easily overlooked. Patients consistently tell us that we are not quite as good at the art of medicine as we are with its science. We must live with this critique and change. As we do, more patients will be healed.

A nurse shared the following story:

When I was a little girl, we moved into a home we knew we would live for only a year. Yet, as soon as we arrived, my mother started cleaning and painting as if there were no tomorrow. She put us all to work.

"But Mom," I said, "We are only going to be here a little time. Why are we doing this?"

Her response was simple, "We are going to leave this place a little better than we found it."

That is what being a healing presence means—leaving others a little better as a result of our care.

Today, I will be aware of how I can be a healing presence by extending my heart and my hand to all I meet. I will leave my work place a little better than I found it.

ommunity

The Physical Medicine and Rehabilitation Department scheduled a meeting of its entire staff this morning. Fifty employees from different hospitals within the system were present. The meeting began in a windowless room as the sun rose.

At the beginning of the meeting, the director of the department had everyone stand in a circle. She then invited the new employees to step forward and form an inner circle. She acknowledged the contributions of each individual to the care of patients.

By doing this she awakened an undeniable feeling in all of us who were present that we were a community of linked individuals with different competencies and gifts. We could easily see that this department could not function without each member's contribution.

The community within a hospital has a special strength because it is built around the common purpose of saving lives, healing bodies and giving comfort. The sacred work we do allows patients to return home to watch their grandchildren grow, gives the promise of mobility to amputees, and sends cancer into remission for countless patients. We are, all of us, a community of healers and we must never lose sight of that. When people come together with a common vision to improve the health of the community, this shared higher purpose generates its own light. The "sunrise" in that windowless room was as real and as significant as the one that welcomed a new day outside.

I will remember that I'm part of a community of healers. I will look for the special energy that is created through our common purpose.

$\mathcal{B}$eing Open to New Ideas

There are over 6 billion people on the planet and all of us thinks we are "right" when we face more than one approach or way to view a situation. This does not exactly set the stage for effective teamwork.

Yesterday, three employees were having an informal discussion in the hallway. I knew one of the three. As I passed by, she reached out and grabbed my arm. "Do you have a minute? We're talking about the need to have a welcoming spirit when working." She was forceful enough that even if I were busy, I would have stopped.

"We don't think it is enough to think of it as being pleasant with one another. We think a welcoming spirit should include welcoming the different ways of thinking about things."

One of the nurses asked the other, "Do you think that welcoming another's thought is the same as respecting another's way of thinking?" The third said, "No, there's a huge leap between the two! If you simply respect another's perspective, you stay trapped in your own little world. There is no real connection. If you welcome another's way of thinking into your own—see as they see—there is a chance that her perspective will change you." Then, the one who had cornered me asked, "So, what do you think?"

Those three nurses were speaking of a problem that philosophers have struggled over for centuries, namely, how do we quiet our own way of thinking long enough to genuinely understand the perspective of another. Indians refer to this challenge when they encourage us to walk in the moccasins of others before criticizing. That gift involves the ability, in the midst of a conversation, to ask someone to explain her position and not simply advocate for our own.

Our medical facilities serve all kinds of people from all walks of life. When they enter our facilities, they bring their own values, perspectives and cultural norms. If we are not open to their point of view because we're too locked into our own beliefs and agendas, then we are setting ourselves up for misunderstanding. By sticking doggedly to our point of view, we end up filtering the other person's words and actions through our fixed lens. As a result, we are more likely to be in conflict with those with whom we work. However, when we relinquish our need to be "right" all the time, we not only create a more open and welcoming environment for patients and their families, but our personal and professional lives are enriched as we learn more about ourselves, our work, and other cultures.

I will take in the other person's perspective and give it true consideration. That is how I can expand and enrich my values and life experience.

Reflect on the Immense Value of Our Work

Many hospitals have a rich tradition of striving to provide the highest quality of care. A patient's appearance, wealth or condition should not influence the care they receive. Our hospitals are remarkable in this way. Many are even more extraordinary because of their dedication to serve the poor, under-served, and disadvantaged. We do not do this to be recognized.

We often find ourselves so taken up with our everyday responsibilities, that we lose perspective and lose sight of the value of our work. As this occurs, we know that it is time to step back, look at the good we've done, and give ourselves credit for the contributions we've made to other people's lives and to our organization. Affirmations about the work that we or others have done never hurt anyone. In fact, it does the reverse. By reminding ourselves why we went into this work in the first place, we are bound to reconnect with the passion that drew us to this sacred work.

Whatever our jobs, remember that our work directly contributes to the immense good that our organizations provide to those in need. Together, we make a difference.

Today, I will take time out to acknowledge the value of the work I do. I will also recognize my coworkers for their service. Unconditional giving helps those I serve and enriches my life in unseen ways.

Honoring Our Diversity

On Cinco de Mayo, our colleagues of Mexican ancestry gratefully remember the courage of their parents and grandparents who resisted the invasion of their homeland. In our country, we have turned the memory of those heroic individuals into a boisterous holiday. Back home, Mexican families celebrate the day more quietly.

Alongside us in cubicles, hidden in kitchens, and walking our hallways, are phlebotomists, office assistants, nurses, electricians, physicians, plumbers, and techs of Mexican descent. Often we don't notice their cultural heritage because they have adjusted so well into the American way of life. Yet, it's important to acknowledge it because their cultural background is integral to who they are.

One way to celebrate this day is to offer a heartfelt smile or gesture of appreciation to those for whom this is such an important day.

We need a varied and gifted workforce for many reasons. Most importantly, our diversity allows us to give our patients the best care. Walk the floors of our hospitals. Notice those who frequent our offices. The diversity is striking.

For those who celebrate this holiday, thank you. You remind us that every person is valuable and each of us is a gift to the other.

When a particular holiday or tradition comes along, I will acknowledge it to my coworkers and patients whom I know are celebrating. I will honor their tradition and the richness it brings to me and to our work place.

$\mathcal{B}$ecoming Quiet and Listening
to Our Heart

All of us have a quieter side where hopes and dreams, thoughts and feelings, live within our hearts. These are likely what brought us to health care in the first place. To "be professional," some people feel that they must leave this corner of themselves at the door when they come to work. If they are too "authentic," they fear that they'll be viewed as less competent. Unfortunately, leaving a part of ourselves at home can leave us feeling detached from our work; we work in half-hearted ways. We work better when we listen with our hearts. The patient is looking for a nurse who can change an IV, and make a human connection.

Not only do our patients profit when we set aside a moment of quiet in the midst of a busy day to listen to the quiet stirrings within, but so do we. Consider giving yourself the gift of being quiet and going within—especially on a busy day. By listening to the whisperings of your heart, you will honor its messages and serve others in increasingly more effective ways.

After taking time away for reflection, I will work with the energy and urges that come from my heart. My work will come alive with the fullness of feeling and commitment.

Being On a Mission

Military officers are "commissioned." Health care leaders should be as well. The word commission, similar to the word mission, is formed from the Latin word implying someone is sent. Persons with a mission are sent out with the authority to perform a special service. Soldiers are given a mission and sent to carry it out. So are ambassadors. They are sent to represent a country. They do not represent their personal interests but act for those who sent them.

In health care, we have a distinct mission to relieve suffering and restore hope. Our task is predictable in that we are charged with fostering the healing of those entrusted to our care. What is uncharted is the path to this goal.

A commissioning ceremony is an organization's way to send individuals on a mission. While this is not done today, we have to find ways to commission every employee and doctor, not just the administrators.

Many leaders who have a sense of mission live with the conviction that their work is God's work made visible. Not everyone has that understanding of the world or of his or her work. However, we all have a shared desire to create a remarkable organization that fulfills our collective vision. Some days we may see our work simply as a job. But, now and again, as during a commissioning ceremony, we are invited to recognize the idea of participating in a calling that will inspire us to create a world that reflects our dreams.

Today, I will find a moment to appreciate the importance and sacredness of what my work is all about.

$\mathcal{O}$vercoming Cynicism and Betrayal

The bankruptcy of the Enron Corporation made headline news. Some asked how could a large corporation hide its problems so effectively, collapse so quickly, and end so tragically? Others wondered, how could a few employees make fortunes while so many lost their jobs and their life savings? This collapse is particularly confusing because Enron, as with many health care organizations, spoke specifically of having core values that would shape their decisions and characterize their culture, namely integrity, respect, communication, and excellence. Something went terribly wrong.

When an organization violates the trust of its employees, the feeling of betrayal runs deep. Employees lose jobs through no fault of their own, investors lose their life savings, and the public forfeits its faith in the marketplace. We can't change what happened, but we can learn to hold onto our own values irrespective of the decline of others.

When we are children, we have an endearing and unexamined trust in our world. At some point as the years unfold, that taken-for-granted trust will be broken. Someone or something will disappoint us. At that moment, we will know what it means to be betrayed, and yet something inside us still wants to believe. And so we enter adulthood with a certain naïveté, until we see again that we can be betrayed. As adults, we need to take the extraordinary step of striking a balance between naïveté and cynicism.

In that moment of betrayal, we can easily become disheartened. "Everyone is greedy. You can't trust anyone." Whatever the circumstances, we tend to universalize it. If we take that stance, though, we miss an opportunity to cultivate the essential element of trust, which is necessary to any team effort, within any organization. We have to keep our eyes open, yes, yet we must make a conscious choice to avoid cynicism, and be willing to trust again and again. We can choose to reaffirm the goodness of others in order to build a unique, caring work place.

Choosing good over cynicism is an adult task requiring maturity, an expansive world view, and a fundamental drive to follow one's heart.

I will face the adult task of choosing to affirm the goodness of others and trust my coworkers. Cynicism is tiring. Trust is energizing. I can take care of myself and be trusting of others.

Choosing an Attitude of Abundance

This is the holiday season. Hanukkah, the feast also known as the Festival of Lights, has begun. During these days, Jews will commemorate the victory of the Maccabees, the rededication of the Temple at Jerusalem, and the oil that miraculously burned for eight days. For Christians around the world, this is "Advent," a time of waiting for the moment when God's presence, and a recognition of the sacredness of this world, are awakened. The waiting comes to fruition on Christmas Day when their savior is born.

With our 21st century technical savvy, it is hard to accept the seemingly impossible notion in the Jewish legend that a day's worth of oil can burn for eight days. It is just as hard to accept, literally, the Christian stories about a few loaves of bread and fishes multiplying enough to feed crowds or water magically turning into wine to meet the needs of wedding guests.

Yet, the truth underlying these stories is profound. They raise questions about scarcity and abundance because they suggest that very small resources can actually satisfy many people. These stories help us think twice about how we approach the world. We have to wonder if small kindnesses and acts of generosity don't make a bigger contribution than we imagine. If we're operating in a mode of scarcity, we're quick to say no because we feel we don't have enough to give. We are acting on an underlying belief that there's a finite amount of resources, and if we give something away, there won't be anything left for us. When we function with an abundant mentality, we have a certain faith that when we give, we are making an empty space to be filled by something new. In other words, giving promotes abundance, not scarcity.

In the stories, there seemed to be a scarcity of oil, wine, bread and fish. "There's not enough!" people cried. Then, astonishingly, there was plenty.

Do you think it makes a difference if we approach life with an attitude of abundance rather than one of scarcity? Do you think it makes a difference in the way we work? I do. It may influence what we say and even how we respond to patients or colleagues when they ask if we have a moment.

When someone asks for something, whatever that might be, use it to reflect on the perspective from which we view the world. Abundance and scarcity are not simply about wealth. They are about time and every other quantifiable aspect of the human condition.

Am I approaching my work and my life with an attitude of abundance or scarcity? How does my approach affect my response? I will offer more of my time and my self and see how that feels.

Being a Human Being, Not Just a Human Doing

A small group of employees was sitting around a table in the cafeteria informally discussing their concerns. One of the participants was a surgeon who talked about a patient he had operated on several years ago. The woman had returned to speak with him because her cancer had advanced to a stage where current treatments, including surgery, would not work. He felt terrible and helpless knowing that he couldn't do a thing for her.

As he spoke, it was clear to each of us listening, that the patient really did not want him to do anything. She simply needed his presence because she had connected with him and trusted him. It was the surgeon, used to being helpful, who felt he needed to do something.

All of us are challenged to remember that "doing" is only one side of life. There is another side that is harder to describe. Caught up in the everyday world of schedules, deadlines and responsibilities, it is easy to forget the importance of simply being present to one another. This patient, facing mortality, knew better than her physician, the importance of being present to one another.

At times when involved in the workaday world of health care, we can overlook the fact that we yearn for human presence, understanding and acceptance. Curing (doing) is important but so is healing (being). One is not more important than the other. Many times, curing someone is not an option, but it's always possible to heal if we are willing to extend ourselves.

We think this effort will drain us even more at the end of a hard day, but paradoxically, making contact is rejuvenating. To think that we are too busy to make this effort is to miss out on what it means to be human.

My ability to provide healing may come in the form of listening, holding a hand, and truly accepting with an open heart, the feelings and thoughts that someone shares with me. Sometimes, after everything possible has been done, it is this human connection that has the ultimate power to soothe.

Making the Ordinary, Extra-Ordinary

Philosophers remind us that we are irreplaceable—one of a kind. Never again, they say, will there be another you. No wonder talk of cloning makes us nervous.

Our uniqueness is an extraordinary fact that unnerves some, motivates others, and has the ethicists wondering. Because we are one of a kind, and never fully aware of the persons we are called to be, the Spanish philosopher Miquel de Unamuno believes that we need to live with such passion that when we die, others will feel that we should not have died precisely because "no one else can fill the gap that will be left." In order to live up to our potential with such passion, we must be aware of our unique qualities. We cannot fully express that which we have not acknowledged.

If you have a difficult time thinking of yourself as that irreplaceable, take a moment to assume it is true. This may require living "as if." From there, it is a short step to begin doing ordinary things in "extra" ordinary ways. By doing ordinary tasks—nursing care, lab work, cleaning, preparing food, typing letters, maintaining accounts, ordering supplies—in extraordinary ways, we are shaped into the persons we are called to be. That is almost always more than we imagine.

What is true for individuals is equally so for organizations. They are similarly irreplaceable. While constantly being formed, changing, and dying, organizations have histories and identities. If a hospital can realize the unique role it plays in a community, it is challenged to become the organization that has been envisioned. Health care is not merely a business venture; it has a call and responsibility to become the organization that the community needs.

In whatever "ordinary" activities you are involved on this day, think of doing them in "extra" ordinary ways.

Today, I will nurture a heartfelt prayer of gratitude for having a chance to express my talents in a unique, irreplaceable way. I will reflect on what it means to be irreplaceable, and the responsibility I have to live this life with passion, grace and commitment to be the best I can be. I will attempt to do my "ordinary" activities in an extra-ordinary way.

*H*aving a Shared Vision

Is having a vision as important for individuals as it is for organizations? One of our colleagues is a young Native American Ute. Her family had no money. From childhood, she has been overcoming significant obstacles like epilepsy and family poverty. However, from the time she was a child, her mother had her read and reread this short poem.

GOOD, BETTER, BEST. NEVER LET IT REST
UNTIL OUR GOOD IS BETTER, AND OUR BETTER IS THE BEST!

Not only is she our colleague, she is also our teacher, because no matter what happened, she never took her eye off her goal to achieve her absolute best. Even when her path led her into muddy patches, she knew it was part of her journey and she never lost sight of her destination and never lost total faith in her ability to succeed. Deep down, she knew she could—and would—make it, despite the detours, the missteps, and the setbacks.

We all internalize messages from our parents and manifest them throughout our lives. "Rebecca" probably received a lot of messages from her mother—as we all do—but this poem is the one that really took root for her, partly because she sensed how her mother cherished this philosophy. Just as Rebecca embraced her mother's vision, we do the same.

A shared vision is powerful, and when it is about excelling, organizations can make breakthrough results when they are focused on achieving clinical excellence. By being forever mindful of the vision we hold for ourselves, we, too, are destined to achieve the very greatness we have imagined.

What are my inner messages? If the ones I have are not leading me to greatness, I will create and adopt new ones. I believe in the power of a shared vision.

The Life and Death Value of Teamwork

Some time ago, we had a seriously ill patient who was in his sixties. He wasn't a citizen and he did not speak English. He had been admitted to the hospital a few months earlier, received treatment, and then released. I was informed that his debilitating illness would take his life within a year or two.

A few days ago, he arrived in the emergency room, and I received a call to assist at his admission. He hadn't eaten for days and he appeared to be in severe pain, so much, in fact, that he could not be touched. From his disheveled appearance, we concluded that he had not been receiving proper care at home. The patient stayed all day at home alone. His brothers looked after him when they returned from work. A 9-year-old neighbor looked in on him during the day. They were probably all doing the best they could, but clearly, it wasn't enough. The man suffered unnecessarily and the lack of treatment weakened his condition.

The case manager's challenge was determining how to arrange for care at home so he could live out his days in relative comfort.

Technically, once this patient was stabilized, he should have been discharged. However, if we did that, we would be sending him back into the deteriorating situation that had led to his hospitalization. Should we do it? The man was Mexican. Should he be sent back to his homeland where he had no family and no medical care available?

The physician, using the abilities of a particularly sensitive translator, was able to develop a realistic plan to take care of the patient's needs following his hospitalization. The physician and translator went above and beyond the usual call of duty by bringing in social workers, church volunteers, and others who were familiar with his cultural and religious heritage. All of these people worked cooperatively to build a comprehensive plan to ensure he would receive the food, housing and medical attention he needed to live comfortably. In health care, we often see how our ability to act as a well-functioning team has life-and-death consequences.

Most people never see the kind of comprehensive and thoughtful care that this patient received, yet it goes on every day. Unfortunately, we also have examples where teamwork is absent. As a result, patients suffer. We usually don't think of the janitor as playing a part, but what if a patient had an unusually low white cell count and the floor of his room wasn't washed for a few days? What if no one told the janitor this, and his work caused the patient to catch a life-threatening cold? What if nobody told the dietician to withhold solid food before surgery and the patient suffered as a result?

Whenever there is an airplane crash and ensuing investigation, the final report always lists a series of errors that lead to the crash, seldom a single mistake. It is the same with hospitals. Think of a pyramid-shaped building made of children's wooden blocks. Even after one or two blocks have been removed, the pyramid may still look structurally sound. But keep removing the blocks and eventually, the structure will cave in. Sometimes there is a quick collapse, and at other times, there is slow crumbling. But create enough gaps in the building and eventually, it will fall. To keep that from happening, teamwork and excellent communication are required.

To build and sustain a culture of teamwork, each of us must do our part. We must remain consciously committed to open, two-way communication, value the role we play so that we play it to the best of our ability, and accord equal importance and respect to other members of the team, those who prepare food, ready the rooms, maintain the electrical system, and stack the pharmacy shelves. All these jobs might seem less important than the physician's and nurse's work, yet every one of us is needed and is connected to the care of patients. We are partners.

I will look at my teammates with a refreshed sense of appreciation. I will be more aware of being a positive contributor to my team and try to work together for the highest and best outcome for all.

Respecting Inner Struggles

A nurse and former colleague ended her life last week. Death—especially suicide—shakes us because it seems to go against every need we have to nurture and preserve life. The fact that this nurse's death was unexpected made it all the more unsettling. All of us wondered if we could have done more to support her.

Everyone struggles. All of us live closer to the edge than we are aware, and it takes surprisingly little to push us off. A sudden death, a financial blow, a spurned love are enough. Sometimes it may seem as if death is the only option. That's how this nurse may have felt. We don't know. We do know that we were her colleagues for a short time as she struggled to discern how she could best use her talents as a nurse. She did confide in others that emergency medicine was not the best place for her. Perhaps working with people in crisis added a layer of stress that made it impossible for her to find a reason to live.

We all have two sides: professional and personal. Revealing to coworkers our deeply held personal fears seems oddly inappropriate, despite the enormous investment of time and energy we devote to one another at work. Yet, as inner pressures build and the dissonance grows between our inner emotional life and our outer appearance, isolation grows.

Suicide is a lonely act of desperation. We can't force someone to reveal their inner pain, but we can provide an opening and create a receptive environment to lighten their suffering. The simple act of sharing is a way to care, yet it provides no answer to the questions suicide raise.

Today, I will say a little prayer for those who have taken their lives. I will remember that everyone has a side hidden from view.

What Can the Great Religious Traditions Teach Us About Health Care?

Working within health care, it is easy to forget what is happening outside the world of our work place. If we were looking at ourselves from outer space, we would notices millions of people in motion. It is fall and they are celebrating. As we take a closer look, we can see what these great traditions can teach us.

The Jewish community is celebrating Rosh Hashanah. During these ten days of penance, they acknowledge their failings, ask pardon of G-d, and promise to turn again toward others with love. For sins against another person (rather than G-d), they must first seek reconciliation with the offended person and, if possible, right the wrongs committed. For the Jewish people, this is one of their holiest seasons.

The Muslim community is celebrating Ramadan, which involves a month of fasting during daylight hours. When evening falls, they are drawn closer to one another as they eat sparingly with family and friends. During this holiday within Muslim countries, many persons, particularly the young, line the roads to offer water and fruit to those passing by. The practice of offering food to others while hungry oneself, is another way to remember to put others' needs and comfort ahead of one's own. That is curiously close to what we do when we go out of our way to create a welcoming spirit within our organizations.

This week, the Christian community the world over has celebrated the Feast of Francis from Assisi. It is startling that this man is admired almost a thousand years after his death. His appeal lies in his reverence. He recognized that all of creation—the sun, moon, every living creature, and each person—were his sisters and brothers. Most of us remember this prayerful sentiment: Grant that we may not so much seek to be consoled as to console; to be understood as to understand; to be loved as to love.

All three of these holidays offer valuable insights we can take to work. Rosh Hashanah suggests that all of us make mistakes and it underscores the importance of reviewing our actions, asking for forgiveness when we fall short, forgiving ourselves, and forgiving others when they hurt us. While asking for forgiveness may be a humbling experience, it doesn't have to be a humiliating one. Instead, it allows us to feel a sense of closure on what was a hurtful situation, learn from it and move on.

The celebration of Ramadan supports our awareness of the importance of giving to others. While Muslims practice this by giving away food, we can draw from this practice by understanding that in health care, we are offering a service and giving of ourselves. There is great value in putting others' needs ahead of our own.

Through the celebration of the Feast of Francis of Assisi, the Christian community expresses the importance of recognizing the deeper connection that we all have with one another. It is through this understanding that we can better serve others. If we can recognize this truth, we can more easily listen to others and more effectively respond to their needs. In other words, we become better practitioners, more effective team players, and more supportive coworkers. Francis devoutly wanted to be an "instrument" of peace. He was. Because of his words, his presence and his actions, his legend lives on today, and people are still influenced by his ways. Given our mission to foster healing and health, what would happen if we thought of ourselves as "instruments of healing?" How would such a realization impact the way we relate to others, whether patients or colleagues?

Today, I will take a moment to reflect on the larger events taking place outside of my work life. I will respect others' traditions and honor my own.

Seeing Beyond Stereotypes

For a fleeting moment after 9-11, the country was united as if it was one small community mourning its dead. The legacy of that day is perhaps a greater appreciation of life and of one another. We recognize that life is a gift.

For those who think misfortune could never happen to them, consider some of the homeless people standing in line for free meals at parishes around the country that serve thousands of meals every day. Many of them are women and children. If statistics hold true, some of our fellow employees might actually be homeless; they keep it hidden.

You and I are blessed to live in relative security. It's not just that we have a roof over our heads, but we have meaningful work. Our challenge is to avoid feeling entitled.

As we go about our day, we can help ourselves, and each other, by taking a second look at those we meet, particularly patients and strangers. We will not be privy to their life circumstances. We will not even know if they are homeless. Yet a second glance provides an opportunity to move beyond stereotypes to see one another as individuals, not as "them." This is a priceless gift we give to others and to ourselves.

Today, I will see the people I work with and care for as individuals. I will be grateful for the lessons they teach me and enriched by their presence.

How Feverish Activity Keeps Us from Practicing the Art of Caring

Often we are lured into the notion that by simply being busy, efficient, and technically proficient we are doing enough. But that doesn't necessarily mean we are bringing a healing presence to our patients and to one another.

For centuries, philosophers and those in the behavioral sciences observed that feverish activity was actually a symptom of being uninvolved, even though it would seem to indicate over-involvement. Surprisingly, they also found that a person who is truly engaged in an activity does not rush. For example, researchers noticed that little children entering a museum lobby were restless, noisy and difficult to control. When the same children moved from the lobby into the galleries where there were interesting objects to see, they became noticeably less fidgety. They would stop for a moment and then move slowly toward the objects they were attracted to. Their parents did not have to constrain them as they did in the lobby. Researchers came to the conclusion that the children slowed down because they were engaged.

Do you think the world of art has something to teach us about the art of caring? Beyond taking a pulse, replacing an IV, or handing out a pill, we have to pause long enough to recognize the patient as a person in pain, crisis, or in need of our help. This process cannot be rushed. Whenever we hurry, the art of caring is difficult. We may be efficient but what was the patient's experience?

The nature of our work—one that gives us meaning and makes what we do so important—is the person-to-person activity. In order for one individual to make a real connection with another, the process cannot move like a fast-food line. The temptation is always to speed up in an effort to check more things off the to-do list, but we must resist it and slow down enough to do things right. In those timeless moments of connection, we must honor the art of what we do. While it may sound idealistic, perhaps we all need to become artists.

Today, I will notice how a slower pace affects the quality of my work. I will see if I can accomplish what I need to, even while working at a slower pace.

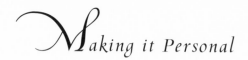

Making it Personal

In hospitals, it's not that uncommon to hear the patient in Room 302 referred to as the "kidney failure case," or one in Room 410 referred to as the "heart transplant." It's understandable that with all of the human heartbreak and suffering we see daily, we tend to protect ourselves from burnout by distancing ourselves and detaching from our patients. Notwithstanding, our work is deeply personal.

One aspect of providing excellent patient care is making patients feel like they are being treated with respect. We do this by making a conscious effort to be particularly sensitive to each patient. It means treating everyone as if he or she were a friend or member of our family. There is little need to share our personal lives with patients but we do need to be personable. When we see patients as individuals rather than a "kidney transplant," we will treat them with respect.

For those of us who do not work directly with patients, look for ways to bring a level of respect and sensitivity to our colleagues by being polite, professional and caring—one person at a time, one situation at a time.

Today, I will make a conscious effort to treat everyone I meet with respect. I will grow from this experience professionally and personally.

Learning from Astronauts

Do you remember sitting in silence watching the memorial service for Columbia's astronauts who died when the shuttle exploded over Texas? The President quoted the wife of the Israeli astronaut who said that her husband was at the peak of his career, doing what he wanted, with the people he loved. She, and all those who loved these astronauts, could at least take some comfort in the fact that they died doing what they loved. I remember the words of Commander Husband; "Being an astronaut isn't a job for me, it's a passion." The loss of the Columbia led many to reflect on the value of having dreams and the importance of contributing to a project that is larger than any one of us.

In a moment of quiet, we can see the parallels between the loss of Columbia and our work within health care. Seven astronauts lost their lives when something unplanned and unforeseen went terribly wrong. Patients also die unexpectedly. Life can end in an instant. Any idea of control that we might have is fleeting. We also note that astronauts work in a certain way; they know that each day can be their last. Think of the passion and aliveness we would feel if we brought this attitude into our work each day. Our lives are not in immediate jeopardy because of the work that we do, but if, as we treated each patient, we carried with us an awareness of the fragility of life, think of how that would heighten the quality of our interactions. If we stayed mindful of the importance of the work that we do and of our unique ability to perform it, if we deeply carried with us the notion that we are truly making a life-altering contribution to our patients, their family, friends and the community in which we live, think of how much more fulfilling and satisfying our work would be.

During the memorial service, current and former astronauts expressed the idea that they and their families were engaged in exploring the universe, and despite its risks, the exploration was well worth taking. They were vocal and explicit about their belief in the sacredness of creation, of what they are about, and the value of their work. We can honestly assume the same view, even though our names won't go down in history.

Today, I will reflect on why I joined the health care profession. I will rekindle the love and passion I have for my work.

Making the Tough Decision to Leave

This morning, our CEO announced his resignation. He had accepted an invitation to be the chief executive of another well-known hospital system. Whenever a colleague chooses to leave, some of us might feel betrayed. We trusted him in his leadership role and believed him as he inspired us to invest our energy, ideas and efforts to reach shared goals for our organization. Others may feel particularly disappointed because that person is such a strong and attractive leader. "We placed our hope in him." Or, we might not be disappointed in his performance as a leader, but feel abandoned by his decision to leave. We trusted his commitment to the organization and now he's chosen to leave. Or, we may feel insecure about his reasons for leaving; does he know something we don't know about our organization's future? Is he abandoning ship and should we polish up our resumés, too?

All of these musings are fodder for talk around the break room where gossip is frequent. The fact is, unless we talk to the person or know her well, we really don't know why someone chooses to make the change. We can take the edge off some of our concerns by considering the perspective of the person leaving. It is helpful to remember that people often make these hard decisions for personal reasons that overshadow the potential fallout that their absence will have on the organization or us, their colleagues and coworkers.

Clearly, this man's decision was not an easy one. On the one hand, we have seen his commitment to the hospital, its patients, physicians and employees. His investment is undeniable: we've felt his passion, we've observed his drive to set the course for our organization in a positive direction. He will not be around to see the fruits of many of his initiatives and hard work, and changing jobs means starting all over again. On the other hand, the invitation to lead one of the country's leading hospitals is not only attractive, but also something of a calling. Perhaps he felt that he had contributed all he could here and it was time to bring his talents to another organization that needed his help. Pulled between the two, it is easy for us see the conflict he experienced. By understanding his perspective and recognizing that there may be a lot of reasons for someone to leave a job, our sense of disappointment will settle to one of sadness at his leaving, and compassion for his decision.

Anyone who is in a leadership position (which includes all of us, since we influence others regardless of our place on the organization chart) may take some comfort in remembering that successful leaders are not effective because they lead others to become dependent on them. On the contrary, they awaken the leadership in the people whom they have inspired, and empower them to join in their cause.

So, while a CEO's decision to leave may have some unique aspects to it, each of us has faced similar conflicts and personal challenges at different times in our lives: the need to live with personal integrity when faced with life-altering decisions. Our choices please many and disappoint some, and awaken intense feelings in others. No wonder philosophers say that an inevitable loneliness accompanies those who strive to move on even when others will be disappointed or disapproving. But a person who has his own sense of mission knows he must follow it. It takes integrity to stay on our own path. Intuitively, in spite of the disappointment, we recognize and value those who develop this depth of spirit precisely because they are willing to pay the cost of making painful decisions.

One philosopher reminds us that we grow in stature and wisdom not when we must choose between good and bad, but when we must choose between two goods.

I will respect the decision that a coworker makes to leave my organization. I will also make my decisions with integrity and follow my calling.

Infusing Our Work with Gratitude

There are many blessings that we take for granted: the comfort of family and friends, the freedom that comes with good health, and the security of having a stable job. The sentiment of gratitude is generated when we reflect on these blessings.

Each of us is a reason for all of us to be thankful. Almost all employees are genuinely grateful for the people they work with, yet we seldom express it. Today is a time to do so.

Why? Kindness and sensitivity to others are sentiments that gather gradually to form a climate conducive to healing. By becoming a healing presence to one another, we avoid burnout, and create a sustainable, nourishing, and enriching place to work.

I will express my gratitude to my coworkers today. I will help create a healing environment wherever I am.

Giving the Gift of Ourselves

Tomorrow is the eve of Christmas. While we scurry for last-minute gifts, we can smell the anticipation in the air. Children can hardly contain their enthusiasm as they wait for the presents they hope to receive and give hand-made treasures to loved ones. As adults, we treasure a hand-made gift from a child who has not yet learned the need to buy gifts.

We can learn from children just as we learn from our patients. Both remind us that many valuable gifts are not purchased. It is easy to over-look the fact that we can be gifts to each other, and that in fact, the gifts that come from the heart, that are crafted and delivered after much thought about the special needs of the recipient, have far more value than the priciest item bought from the trendiest boutique. When we receive a gift that reflects the giver's generosity of time, heart and thoughtfulness, we know it, and we are warmed to the core. What makes these gifts so special is that they respond to the specific, real needs of the person, and aren't just a quick-grab, off-the-shelf obligatory purchase.

What kind of priceless gifts can we give today? Maybe it's making an unexpected phone call that reawakens fond memories, or voicing a genuinely felt goodbye to a patient at the end of a long day, or showing our appreciation to colleagues. If you do not know how to go about this, think of what you could give if you had no money. Think about what your coworkers or patients could use at that moment—something that would lift their spirits, make their day.

The gift you give will likely have immense value because it reflects the extra effort you've made to do something uniquely supportive, with no apparent immediate return for yourself. The special-ness comes from knowing that you've gifted that person with a positive, lasting feeling of being seen, remembered and valued.

Today I will be spontaneous, thoughtful and soulful in my gift giving.

Bringing Artistic Passion to Our Work

Health care professionals feel the need to improve patient care. Sometimes we feel so pressured and are moving so fast that it is difficult to hear the calmer voices and give ourselves this moment of pause.

Another reflection, *Work Differently, Not More*, suggested that "working harder" was not the solution. A more effective approach is to reflect on our dreams when we entered health care. Another way is to look at our work in an artistic way.

While we may not think of ourselves as artists, we are. Artists beautify the world, help us see in new ways, and make the world a better place in which to live. Isn't that what we do?

I read a nurse's note on a patient's chart this morning. It was a masterpiece; clear, accurate, detailed, and informative. I needed some office supplies the other day and entered the supply closet, which was neatly organized and stocked with every item I was looking for. Some unsung artist had taken the time to keep them available, accessible and artfully arranged so I could quickly find what I wanted in no time. I walk down a hallway and into our lobby on marble floors that are polished and sparkling clean. Looking over to the building's doorway, I see an entry that is tracked with water and dirt from the fresh snow—clearly the "before picture" of the now-sparkling floors I am walking on. The fellow mopping and polishing those floors creates a masterpiece even if no one notices, knowing that the shine will last only until morning when it has to be done again. He, too, is an artist, and he works with same sense of impermanence as the artist who creates a Tibetan sand painting: taking enormous time and energy to envision and execute an elaborate design, and an extraordinary level of work to arrange, knowing that the beautiful colored sand will be in disarray tomorrow with one gust of wind. On every floor, within every office, behind every computer, there are artists. Those who think of themselves as artists, approach their responsibilities a little differently than others who are just trying to get through the day.

Let's look at how an actual artist views his own work. The Smithsonian ran an interesting study of creative and productive individuals. They featured a short interview with Tony Bennett, the 79-year-old, 12 Grammy Award winning, popular vocalist. In addition to singing, he loves to paint. One of his works hangs in the Smithsonian Museum. When asked about painting, he remarked, "My whole life I've been painting every day. I've been blessed with the fact that as far back as I can remember, I've always had a passion to sing and paint. I do both, and I don't consider it work!"

This is how we can all think about our work. Do what is counterintuitive in stressful, busy times: take a step back, prioritize the to-do list, stay focused on a vision, and then tap into an artistic passion and energy.

Today, I will bring an artist's perspective and creative energy to my work. I will try to slow down, reduce my stress, reevaluate my priorities and bring more passion to my work. Maybe I won't even consider what I do as work!

$\mathcal{F}$acing the Questions that Death Brings

Last week, we were saddened by the sudden death of our colleague, Martha. The fact that she died so unexpectedly contributed to our bewilderment. Members of her department arranged a sensitive memorial service. I will not forget the faces of her children. Who can fathom the unexpressed feelings of a 13-year old daughter who has just lost her mother? Who could be untouched seeing her teenage son sitting stoically?

I had lunch with an employee who was affected by this woman's death even though she only knew her in a limited way. They merely attended the same meetings on occasion. Here's what she told me:

I noticed that when we had a meeting this week, the chair in which Martha sat was empty. It seemed no one wanted to sit in it. I also noticed that during the meeting, we picked up with the work that had to be done. Martha's absence didn't slow us down. I don't think people are callous. They were affected by her death, but they kept their feelings to themselves. This was the time for work.

I couldn't help thinking, "If I died, would these people continue on as if nothing happened?" The whole experience made me wonder if I am really as valuable to the organization as I think I am.

She appeared to be questioning whether or not all the hours we devote to work are worth it if the void of our death can be filled so easily. She and her colleagues seemed to place more of an emphasis on getting things done rather than acknowledging a coworker. Was this a balanced perspective?

I also told myself, "We've got to find a way to have a more balanced way of seeing this." I found myself thinking about life in general, that if I lived a more balanced life, I had to wonder if I would work as hard as I do now. I don't like thinking that way because I am really committed to the effort to become the best at what we do.

As she thought about it, she second-guessed her decision not to attend the memorial service on Saturday afternoon, yet she really couldn't make it. She looked for a solution that would help people like her who were caught between two important choices.

This led me to think that I would appreciate a hospital-wide celebration or memorial service now-and-again during work hours because then I wouldn't have to choose between work and remembering a colleague, which are both equally important, but in different ways. I only knew Martha in passing. Martha's death is making me think that we are missing something if we don't have a way to acknowledge significant events in our lives. Death is surely one of those.

Perhaps it is actually easier for some people to just work harder than to face the death of someone who has worked among them. However, by doing that, we are left with a feeling that something significant is missing. When someone we know dies, rather than avoid the thoughts and feelings that surface, we can embrace them and allow ourselves to open to a new perspective that death invites us to consider.

I will embrace the large questions that death suggests I examine. Facing them allows me to enrich my life experience.

Believing Is Seeing

When one of our seasoned employees learned of this year's goal to improve patient satisfaction, she quipped, "Can't be done. I'll believe it when I see it." She lives by the maxim "seeing is believing." If they reach the goal, then she'll believe the goal was reachable. She was standing back as an observer, not a participant.

In newspaper accounts of Lance Armstrong's remarks about the attitude needed to excel, he says, "It's a question of believing." If he hadn't had an extraordinary belief in his own capacity, he would never have driven himself to win the Tour de France a record seven times in a row. Instead of embracing a wait-and-see attitude, he was inclined to first believe in what might be, and then to tenaciously work to make that dream a reality.

Believing in the goodness of others, the value of caring, the importance of our jobs, and the sacredness of our work, helps us to work towards those ideals. It means we can summon the energy to achieve them and become the organization we envision. All of this calls for a remarkable faith.

Those we admire have known this all their lives. Think of Martin Luther King Jr.'s sentiment when he set out to follow a seemingly unreachable dream, "Faith is taking the first step even when you don't see the whole staircase."

I will create the work place I desire by visualizing it and taking the first step toward this new reality. I will replace disbelief with action.

Acting with Gratitude

Look around. There is plenty to be grateful for. Look with the eyes of gratitude, and we will find more and more to appreciate. Operating with gratitude refreshes our perspective and it takes what was once routine and tedious and makes it come alive.

Gratitude does something to the human heart. Rather than withdraw to protect our blessings, we experience an awakened sense of responsibility and a desire to be of help to others. When we live with gratitude, every act is influenced.

In the hospital, gratitude helps us see every patient as a gift. Each one provides us with an opportunity to practice our skills and to stretch us emotionally. We express our gratitude through our interactions and through the quality of care. At the end of the day, we can be eternally grateful that we have fulfilling work.

Today, I will make a gratitude list. I will be gratefully aware of the gifts that come from my patients, coworkers and others who come into my life.

Living the Life We've Been Given

The hospital chapel was overflowing with people attending the memorial service for one of our IT employees. How had they been able to arrange their work to make time for the service? How could so many employees know a man who worked in a cubicle except for the rare times he left it to assist others with their computer problems?

The numbers were so striking that I could not resist asking them why they had come. Their answers were remarkably similar. They wanted to be there because they had such a heart-felt connection to him. Many employees used the same three words: he was *pleasant, competent* and *responsible*. I was struck by the emphasis placed on his being pleasant because a person who works in IT is usually under considerable pressure to fix problems immediately, which doesn't put most people in a very "pleasant" mood. Dealing daily with demanding clients requires an extraordinarily calm, patient manner. As to his competencies and reliability, one manager said, "If you asked him to do something, you could be sure he would follow through. In the department we used to say, 'Don't worry, Ennis is on it.'"

Ennis died unexpectedly and young. Perhaps the ancient Greek philosophers were right when they taught:

> THERE IS NOT A SHORT LIFE OR A LONG LIFE.
> THERE IS ONLY THE LIFE THAT YOU HAVE,
> AND THE LIFE YOU HAVE IS THE LIFE YOU ARE GIVEN,
> THE LIFE YOU WORK WITH.
> IT HAS ITS OWN SHAPE, DESCRIBES ITS OWN ARC, AND IS PERFECT.

When somebody dies, it tends to draw the living into a reflective mood. We find a minute to draw apart for a while and recognize the arc of our own lives. Then we return to the work at hand with an increased appreciation of its value, as well as its sacredness.

How will I be remembered when I die? How I am as a person today is the legacy I will leave when I'm gone.

Finding Meaning in Volunteerism

Why would a 40-year old lawyer in the midst of a busy practice volunteer her time so consistently?

Why does a state official volunteer weekly to visit patients in one of our hospitals?

We have a completely voluntary Board of Directors. Why do those remarkably successful women and men volunteer their time without any compensation?

Why did one of our employees raise $25,000 dollars for an inner city health clinic by finding individuals to sponsor her climb up one of Europe's highest peaks?

Why do some of our physicians volunteer their services to hospitals and clinics in developing countries year after year? Not only do they forego their income from work at home, but they pay their own way to those far away countries.

Why does one of our nurses work six months in Africa and six months in one of our emergency rooms? Why does another nurse volunteer her time after work (along with her teenage children) to paint rooms in the city's largest homeless shelter?

Do people who contribute to developing nations do so because they want to travel and see the world? If they wanted that, they could take a cruise ship.

Are those in our own town who reach out to others in remarkably generous ways merely condescending do-gooders proud of their generosity? Not likely.

In the spirit of volunteerism, we recognize that the whole world is our family, and we open our hearts to tend to them as we would our own children. Not only is it the right thing to do, it fills a void in us, too. There is a deep human need for meaning and connectedness and knowing that you can make a unique contribution to people you may never meet again.

The poet Gerard Manley Hopkins was right when he wrote that within the human heart lives a "dearest freshness."

The physician, Albert Schweitzer, also made it clear when he said that what he did with his life was not unique. Here's what he had to say:

"You may think it is a wonderful life my wife and I have in the equatorial jungle. That is merely where we happen to be. But you can have a still more wonderful life by staying where you happen to be and putting your soul to the test in a thousand little trials, and winning triumphs of love. Such a career of the spirit demands patience, devotion, daring. It calls for strength of will and determination to love: the greatest test of a man. But in this hard 'second job' is to be found the only true happiness."

I will look for ways to make a contribution that will help other people. It is not as important for others to see my efforts, as it is for me to help those in need. I will be a happier person, too.

Reflecting on Life and How We "Show Up" for Work

The end of the year is a natural time for reflection. How did the year, month, week, or day go for us? What were our successes? Did we meet life's challenges with grace or could we improve our responses to disappointment, stress and upheaval?

In centuries past, monks would stop their daily activities at the end of each year and "retreat" for three days to take stock. They thought long and hard about the shortness of life. This was not a morbid practice where they became preoccupied with death. Instead, reflecting on the passing of time awakened an appreciation of life and helped them regain perspective on their lives as monks.

While being a monk carries its own difficulties, it does present the luxury of being free from many of the burdens that householders and employees have to carry—paying bills, replacing the blown-up microwave, handling the complexity of intimate relationships, juggling equally demanding priorities, making our way through traffic, waiting in line for everything when there's not enough time for anything. When you're a monk, your whole focus can be on reflection. When you live in the world, however, you have to carve out the time for reflection and make a conscious choice to do it. In spite of the innate difficulties, it's important to make this a priority. Pulling back a little from our daily activities can help us re-appreciate the richness of our life, and how we've changed emotionally and even spiritually since our last "check in."

Take some time to step back from your daily activities and review your life, especially how you "show up" for work. What does your attitude and behavior say about how you feel about life, love, service and caring? Are these the messages you want to convey? There are people who really do have a good heart, but their crabby disposition keeps others from seeing it. You may know that you have a good heart and that you are a caring person, but is it showing? Sometimes only deep contemplation will reveal to you a painful truth about whether or not there is a disconnect between your inner desire to be a caring person and the personality quirks that seep out because you are too tired, too stressed, and too overwhelmed. A regular routine of reflection can help us realign our inner desire with our outer expression at work.

What do I need to do differently to be a true expression of my values? Regular reflection will become a part of my life. I am grateful for my life and hopeful about the future.

Updating Our Labels

Several years ago when I was a practicing psychologist, I had the privilege to be invited into a monastery as a consultant. The abbot wanted help on how to deal with a problem. Some time ago, one of the monks had decided to leave the monastery to return to lay life. He had been a baker for almost ten years. The abbot said that he always thought of the man as someone who had quite limited talents and that working in the kitchen was about the only job he could do well.

The abbot had to question himself. The man he thought of as "limited" started his own bakery after leaving the monastery. One bakery soon became two, then five, and finally twelve. From there, he was recruited to run an established regional bakery. Three years later, he became CEO of a national chain.

The abbot said, "Inside these walls, I think we put one another in boxes. I can't help thinking something is wrong with the way I treated him." He realized the limitations he was placing not only on other people, but on himself. While this awareness was not a comfortable one, it was his wake-up call to change.

The monk was so much more than a baker. Perhaps that is why he left the monastery. Few can tolerate being in a box for long.

All of us tend to put people in boxes. When we do this, the person being judged must ultimately leave the situation in order to have the freedom to live up to his potential and feel valued. In building a thriving organization, the last thing we want to do is lose valuable, motivated, and talented people. We must create an environment where all valued employees can live up to their potential.

But there is another victim in this judging game: us. When we prejudge people, we hardly realize that we also place restrictions on ourselves. We are not only confining the "boxed" person's ability to contribute, but we are restricting the gifts or results that we and our organization can receive from that person. The wise person learns to think twice about everyone and everything.

I will look at my coworkers with fresh eyes and see the new gifts they embody. I will also let go of the box I've built around myself, try new things, offer new ideas and be all that I can be.

Reflecting on Our Lives in and Outside of Work

Around our national holidays like Memorial Day and Independence Day, we think of the price of freedom: the loss of life that others sacrificed so that we may be free to pursue our passions in our free time.

Social researchers remind us that whatever we do outside of work finds its way into how we work. One of our employees sings in the chorus of our city's symphony orchestra. Others take time to walk quietly before the workday begins. Some jog or work out in another way. Others meditate, read an inspiring book, play an instrument or work with clay. While we can't measure the impact any of this has on our work, outside interests bring a renewed energy to the workday.

There is value in living with intention and cultivating interests outside of work. Everyone profits, including our patients and colleagues. They know the difference between those who go about their work mechanically and those who bring a healing presence. And we know that when we find ways to live a balanced life, we will also work in a balanced way.

How do I spend my life outside of work? I will look for ways to enrich my outside life and to live and work more deliberatively. My life is richer when I take time to reflect on it and then live it with greater awareness.

Using Performance Assessments to Improve Ourselves

When an organization is undergoing a review by the Joint Commission, everyone feels the increased energy and the apprehension as outsiders assess performance. Whether JCAHO does a review on our organization, or our boss reviews our job performance, most people don't look forward to the process. It tends to make them nervous. They may feel judged or simply apprehensive about facing an evaluation. That's understandable. Nevertheless, we have to remember that this process isn't meant to make us feel like a child being called into the principal's office. It is just one part of the important process of continual improvement. We can't change for the better unless we are open to learning and honest feedback, and to the possibility that our feelings may be hurt.

There are ways to prepare for a performance review. Try setting aside time to reflect honestly, with some measure of detachment, on the past year's accomplishments and shortfalls. Writing helps clarify and objectify lessons to be learned. What was accomplished? Where did we fail? Where is there room for improvement? After looking back, look forward. What would we like to achieve or how would we like to change the way we perform our jobs? What do we need, either in our own development, or from others, to reach our new goals? Looking at performance assessment as a time to improve, and supervisors as coaches, changes the assessment process. When we meet with common goals of helping one another to become better at all that we do, it creates a calming, productive atmosphere in which to have a heartfelt, meaningful conversation.

When we complete a performance review, we've learned more about ourselves and we are committed to improvement. It's time to pause and acknowledge our progress. If this performance assessment went more smoothly than past ones, that's something to celebrate. Being open to feedback opens the door to professional improvement and personal growth, which is a benefit to us all.

I will see an assessment as one tool that can help me improve. I will try to welcome the feedback as necessary to being my best.

The Sacredness in the Ordinary

The following is a 15th century, Muslim story:

A farmer was planting his crop when he was told that God was coming to earth at that very moment. Unmoved, he looked down at the work at hand, and continued to plant. The farmer didn't look up or move because he found no need to leave his place to find God.

The story is a reminder that work has a sacredness about it, as mundane as it may seem.

Day in and day out, we are immersed in the bustle of hospital life, of nursing homes, physician offices, and treatment centers. We are bombarded by incessant demands and activities. In the midst of it all, take a moment to listen to quieter voices—not unlike the farmer, who listened but continued to hoe the fields, all the while feeling God's presence.

During these moments, we are mindful of the sacredness of what we are about. At the same time, we might recall the delicate dreams that first led us into health care. Those early hopes and dreams are easily forgotten if we don't continue to nourish them.

Today, I will see the sacredness in my every day work. I will give "air time" to the dreams that drew me into health care and allow them to express themselves in my every day interactions at work.

Respect: Taking a Fresh Look

Some employees say that they do not feel respected by their managers. The word respect is derived from two Latin words, *re* and *spectare*. *Spectare* means "to look" and *re* means "again." So, to respect someone we have to take a second glance, to look again, and to see the other person afresh.

When we see others who have "menial" jobs, it's so easy to overlook their presence and importance. It's also possible to dismiss a CEO, believing that she is hypocritical or out of touch with the organization. Remember, we're only seeing one side of the person, and so our judgment is bound to be superficial. To show respect, we have to take the time to look at one another.

What applies to colleagues also applies to patients. Developing respect for one another involves taking the time to view them from differing perspectives. The unwashed patient or gruff colleagues are more than unwashed and gruff. It takes a second look to discover what lies beneath the surface.

The more difficult challenge is to turn a respectful glance toward ourselves, to drop the boxes in which we have placed ourselves, and then turn outward to care for others. We are always more than we have settled for.

Just as I don't want to be forever labeled, I will look at my colleagues and others with a fresh perspective. I will look beyond appearances and first impressions and respect the individual beneath the surface.

Being Open to the Unseen

Do you feel like playing a game? Count the number of "F"s in the following text.

FINISHED FILES ARE THE RESULT OF YEARS OF

SCIENTIFIC STUDY COMBINED WITH THE

EXPERIENCE OF YEARS

STOP. Do not read further until you have counted.

How many did you count? If you noticed three, you are wrong. There are six. Most people miss the "F"s in the word of.

How often do we miss seeing what is right in front of us because we weren't expecting it? For example, a doctor saw a female patient who was complaining of heartburn and tiredness. He had seen many patients with these symptoms over the years so he assumed she was suffering from the same basic ailment as everyone else—stress. He prescribed a change of diet and told her to learn to care for herself. When she returned a few weeks later however, she had the same symptoms, only worse. This time, she saw the physician's partner. After a more careful examination, the second physician recognized that the woman was suffering from heart disease. Why did the first physician miss the diagnosis? He jumped to conclusions. Said another way, he did not give a second glance. He was not *re*-spectful.

Being a professional, it is easy to think of our beliefs and judgments as "right." However, experts frequently demonstrate a more limited insight than someone with less education but an open mind. Arrogance and self-satisfaction can lead the best of us to overlook what's under our nose. When the truth catches up to us, it can be a very humbling experience.

All of us are subject to this kind of complacency. The first step is to be aware of it. Then, we have to have the humility to put aside our own assumptions and take a fresh look. It will save someone's life.

We can improve the value we bring to our work by being open to what we do not see. A faint discoloration in an x-ray or the slight irregularity of a heartbeat is easy to miss. Respect and humility are key needs for every clinician.

Although humbling, I realize that I may not see everything that's in front of me. Now is an opportunity to learn from others and to be open to new solutions.

*I*ntegrity in Action

During a meeting this afternoon, an employee mentioned how a physician's behavior in one of our emergency departments unsettled her. In the course of a surgery, a time filled with tension, she was the object of his anger. The staff overheard his outburst.

Later, he came up and apologized to her. "I'm sorry for what I said. The truth is, I was preoccupied with something else and I took my frustration out on you."

"That physician has integrity," she told us at the meeting. "When he took personal responsibility for his actions instead of blowing off his behavior, he showed real strength of character and I genuinely respected him for that. I appreciated not only that he was honest with me, but that he had the strength to admit what he had done."

Like the physician, each of us has said or done something that we later regretted, and like him, we can right the wrong. We don't have to let stand the last lamentable words we said. Others will feel better if we make an effort to heal the wounds. It's easy to say that we hold ourselves to a high moral standard, but the real test of this is whether our actions back up our words. How many of us read about leading a more principled life but fail to bring theory into practice? This effort takes on genuine meaning when we bring our values into the work place. When we take personal responsibility for our actions, we shape the place we work into an environment we can be proud of.

I will take a fresh look at my organization's values and think about how I can put those values into practice and shape how I work—as an individual and as a team member.

Remembering the Trust that Others Give Us

Here is an account of the experience of ambulance drivers in New Orleans transporting patients during hurricane Katrina. The New York Times reported:

"At Touro Infirmary, mothers were just giving my medics their little day-old babies. They were just looking at us with fear and horror on their faces. We would put four of them in an incubator and just fly them out. They're scattered all over the country now. We couldn't keep track of where everyone was going."

Can you imagine the experience of those mothers? It seems incredible that they would entrust their newly born infants to strangers. Can you picture how the medics felt as they held those babies? The intensity must have been extraordinary.

On the one hand, there is little comparison between the experience of these people and ours. On the other hand, we do have something in common. Every time a parent, child or friend brings their loved one to the hospital, clinical practice or residential center, they place their trust in us, similar to the way those mothers entrusted their infants to the medics. They don't know us, but they trust us. Often, we are not aware of what an intense and remarkable relationship we are in when we welcome a patient into our care. It can easily seem like one more person among so many.

Events like Katrina shock us into thinking again about our relationship to patients and their families. Whether we are a medic, doctor, nurse, admissions clerk, receptionist, telephone operator, pharmacist, billing clerk, chaplain, buyer, or case manager, we are trusted and needed. If we can keep the image of those mothers handing over their infants in the forefront of our memory—think of them being handed to us—we will recognize the importance of our work and the trust being placed in us, whatever our job. This will influence how we work.

I will reflect on the sacred job I have as others entrust me to help them as only I can. I will encourage my colleagues to find a protected moment of quiet to consider the important role they play.

Honoring Mentors, Being a Mentor

Mr. Rogers of television fame, was fond of saying to children, "All of us have special ones who have loved us into being." He would then invite the children to think of the people who have helped them become who they are. His reason for doing this was to awaken an awareness of being loved and secure.

In the workaday world, we seldom talk of love, but many of us remember special individuals who have helped us become who we are. Often, it is because they said or did something to affirm their belief in our abilities. They were probably our former teachers, supervisors, grandparents, aunts or uncles. When someone has affirmed us profoundly, we carry a memory of them in hidden corners of our mind for years. The more we recognize and appreciate how they helped us, the more we are willing to care for others in similar ways.

If we want to help build an exemplary organization, we have to find ways to transform our treasured memories into the way we work. Practically speaking, that means developing a climate within the work place where affirmation, approval, trust and support are characteristics of every floor, office, cubicle, and conference room.

I will reflect on the important mentors in my life. I will honor them and their efforts by doing my best, and mentoring someone else the way I was so lovingly mentored.

Seeing the Saints Among Us

During the television coverage of the events surrounding the pope's death, the lead commentator expressed his surprise at how many non-Catholics waited in line to pass by his body. "For some reason," he added, "this leader attracted a wide array of people for causes I find difficult to explain."

One explanation may lie in Pope John Paul's own words. As he aged, he knew that every human being is made in the image and likeness of God, and must be treated with dignity. Fame, wealth, poverty, faith, age, appearance, or talents—all of these are of little consequence. Perhaps he appealed to such a wide group of people across cultures because he saw the goodness of everyone. All of us need to be accepted, listened to, and appreciated for what and who we are. Unfortunately, we don't do this nearly enough. We marvel when we see those who do.

Centuries earlier, another man had a similar appeal. Legend has it that Francis of Assisi awakened to the dignity of others when he saw a leper walking toward him on a narrow road. Instead of crossing to the other side to avoid the man, he was moved to embrace him. That was the moment that Francis discovered that the leper was Jesus in disguise. From that point on, it is said that he began to recognize the dignity of every individual.

Why does the memory of Francis linger today? Because we all yearn to be in the presence of those who see the beauty in everyone.

There are saints among us. Observe the way a nursing assistant washes a patient who has soiled his bed when unable to control his bowels. Notice how a tech approaches a patient who has to expose herself embarrassingly in the process of having a mammogram. You will see the difference between employees who simply do their job and those who are saintly.

Look around during a meeting and listen to the words of others. Listen to the way they speak, and you will notice that there are other St. Francis's among us.

The physician, Albert Schweitzer wrote, "You don't have to be an angel to be a saint." We can see the saintly quality in others when they bring a healing presence to the work place.

Today, I will look for the saints around me. I will observe how they see the sacredness in other people and try acting this way, too.

It's Easy to Make a Difference

An acknowledgement can be as simple as a smile or a nod. Our state of mind improves, and our whole day can turn around by the kind words of recognition by a coworker or manager. It doesn't cost anything to extend ourselves in this way and it can have a lasting impact.

The contemporary American philosopher Francis Fukuyama makes a case for the fact that all of us yearn to be acknowledged. "The struggle for recognition is the motor that drives human history."

We can try to be recognized in many ways. Doing a good job is certainly one. I know that I feel better when my good work is acknowledged. While it's a subtle feeling that is often hard to admit, all of us are uncomfortably vulnerable when we are not acknowledged on the job. This is true even for an administrator who is not recognized by a passing physician, or a food service employee who is not recognized by her manager. Since we know how much it means to have our work affirmed, let's not be afraid to give it freely to others. It could be a turning point in their day.

Patients need to be affirmed. They are particularly vulnerable because they are ill. They may also be feeling off-balance as they wrestle with the uncertainty of not knowing when or even if they will return to health. Their lack of control over their illness and their future can leave them feeling decidedly insecure. Feeling as if no one else can understand what they are experiencing can make them feel worse.

Family members are equally vulnerable and needy of affirmation. When a sensitive nurse, lab tech or LPN provides a smile, the family is touched. Not receiving a simple acknowledgement makes people feel unseen.

See how easy it is to extend yourself by affirming the presence of those you meet and observe how your smile and acknowledgment affects them (and you!).

My day will improve as I seek to improve the lives of others.

Resisting New People, New Ideas

During my lunch hour, I went to the pharmacy to pick up some aspirin. When crossing the parking lot, I met one of our nurses walking with her young daughter.

"Say hello to Mr. Helldorfer," her mom said. The child kept her head down with her hands in her pockets. "Oh, go ahead, say hello to Marty. Shake his hand." The child didn't budge. "What's wrong with you? Take your hands out of your pockets."

Slowly, the little girl took her curled right hand from her trousers. Guess what those fingers clutched. A Hershey chocolate kiss! No wonder she did not want to shake hands.

When driving back to work, I wondered if all of us are not, at times, like that beautiful child. What do we cherish most? We might say our privacy, our reputation, and the esteem of others. How many of us hold these things so dear that we won't take the chance of revealing our innermost feelings and dreams to others? One difference between the child and ourselves is that we have grown much more sophisticated in what we hold on to.

Meeting that child has made me think about what holds us back from reaching out to patients and colleagues. The answer will be different for each of us. It is worth pondering.

In this moment of quiet, I will honestly ask myself, "What is holding me back from opening up to others? What am I afraid of losing? What do I have to gain?"

Honoring What's Important and Being Present

When I was a new executive at a large health care organization, I wanted to introduce myself to the nursing home's administrator, but her assistant told me that she was not in her office. Nor was she sitting at the nursing station where the telephone operator thought I would find her. A few moments after being paged, I saw a woman coming across the foyer, hand extended, saying, "Welcome, I recognize you."

Before I could respond she said, "A resident here just died, and his wife has arrived. She needs someone now, and I don't want to leave her alone. This isn't a good time to talk. Would you want to come down with me to be with her?"

This was a wonderful example of patient care. She put the family's needs first instead of relying on protocol. Even though we'd just met, she didn't simply engage in small talk, pretending to listen while she was really preoccupied with the pressure of another crisis down the hall. She found a way to greet me and include me in her work all at the same time. I felt welcomed and I'm sure the family felt cared for.

This administrator's gift is the gift of many engaged in health care. She was able to prioritize the needs of many, while still attending to all. In this case, the necessity of the family trumped organizational expectations. All of us can receive inspiration from her and ponder how we can behave the same way as we face these choices in our work lives.

Today, I will think about what is most important at that moment. I will give my attention first to the care of those who need me.

Valuing Creativity and Play

In the weeks leading up to Halloween, children's minds are imaginative as they think about what costumes to wear and what creature they will become as soon as the sun goes down. While they prepare for Halloween, they are testing themselves and thinking creatively about who they might turn into. It's an exciting process. For many children, the big thrill is seeing adults react to their new-found identities, whether they are princesses, soldiers or goblins.

Children are unique ambassadors representing the land of energy, creativity and play. They play and get us to play and laugh as only the young can do. It sometimes takes quite an effort to drop the adult façade that we've built over the years. After all, we think that as adults, we must be more serious and abandon "play time" in favor of activities that meet our growing obligations. As we age, playfulness may become more difficult to awaken. Creativity may take a back seat to duty. Deep inside there resides a hidden ability to play and be creative.

Children have special qualities to offer those of us in health care. Our work requires enormous energy and creativity. We can change the mood of a patient's room simply by an understanding or welcoming expression on our face. People lying in hospital beds are feeling particularly vulnerable. What an unexpected and invaluable gift we give them just by approaching them with a buoyant attitude and presence.

It's often difficult to imagine that an attitude of play is necessary within hospitals, hospices or skilled nursing facilities. We think of them as places where people are pre-occupied daily with illness, dying and death. Finding a way to lighten things up actually contributes to healing in our patients, and staves off burnout in us. We intuitively understand the healing qualities of play. Play has a way of energizing people—that goes for patients, their families, and us. And once again, we can learn from children. They crave play.

Just by being around children, we are lifted by their spirit and reminded of the value of play without abandoning our responsibilities as adults. No matter how busy we feel we are, we can still find ways to try on new costumes, new ways of doing our jobs, and new and creative approaches to providing high quality health care. Having the freedom to implement new ways of doing things is critical if we want to become the organization we envision.

By being open to a more playful and creative approach to work, I will have more energy and I may discover a new and effective way to do my job. I will let my inner desire for fun come out.

Improving Care One Person at a Time

I have a tendency to stress what is positive in life rather than focus on what is negative. This was strengthened during my clinical training when my supervisors encouraged me to listen intently to the negative but to affirm the positive. I have found that advice particularly helpful over the years.

This week, that approach was challenged when I received a copy of this unsettling note from a patient. He wrote:

"I have been in quite a few hospitals as of late, and generally speaking, the staff [at your hospital] was very unfriendly. I don't think any of them know how to say, 'Hi, how are you?' I don't think they have to fall all over patients, but at least [they need] to act friendly and try to cheer a patient up. [The first one I met] was a classic. He should have been working at a funeral home. I think your hospital staff needs PR [training]."

It wasn't easy to receive a letter like this, but it motivated us tremendously to be more welcoming to patients and their families. These letters remind us of our desire to treat every patient and all of our colleagues in personable and caring ways.

One important component in the way many medical facilities measure success is by the degree of patient satisfaction. How patients feel about the care they are receiving starts with first impressions. Taking the time to look a patient in the eye, say hello, and ask them how they feel is an ongoing challenge when we are busy. Completing tasks always seem more important than making a welcoming gesture. One way to encourage us to extend a warm gesture, is to become genuinely aware of how we affect others. Making people feel welcome sets the tone for the rest of the care we will be giving them. It is as important as taking vital signs, administering medications, and charting.

I will listen to every person I meet and respond as best I can. I will draw from my inner reserve where my needs have been met and be a source of hope and comfort. Every interaction today is sacred.

Waking Up!

Several years ago, I attended a conference and heard a physician tell this true story. I do not remember which conference it was nor the name of the impressive speaker. I have not forgotten the story. A depressed OB/GYN had lost his enthusiasm for his profession. One morning while he was assisting a woman in childbirth, he had a breathtaking experience.

He was holding her newborn in his left hand, and with his right hand he was performing a procedure to suction the mucus from the infant's mouth and nose. He had done this hundreds of times throughout his career. This time, however, the newborn child suddenly opened her eyes. As their eyes met, he became overwhelmed by the realization that he was the first human being this baby ever saw. He was filled with an overwhelming sense of obligation to welcome her into the world.

The experience had a remarkable impact on this man. He didn't leave the profession after all, but "awoke" to what caring for others was all about— the unique impact that all health care professionals have to support life, and to be there for others when they're at their most vulnerable. He remains in his practice today.

Every day, we have an opportunity to awaken to the value and importance of what we do. Even after years of sleepwalking through our work, we can wake up one morning and become conscious of the affect we have daily on the lives of the people we meet. Moments of awakening influence how we work, why we work and how we spend our time throughout the day.

Every time my eyes meet those of my patients, my colleagues, my friends, my children and my loved ones, I will see this as an invitation to awaken to this special moment and to the unique gifts I have to offer.

Being Open to New Ideas

Sometimes in daily life we expect one thing, yet find another. We learn by being open to the unexpected. After all, if we expect something, we already know it! Expectations simply reinforce what we already know. Real learning begins with inquiry. True learners are wide open to new perspectives and fresh ideas; they possess a genuine eagerness to know more.

Learning is a gift. Children have it and so do many adults. The gift is easy to lose as we grow older. Likely, there are many reasons for this. Some people have a physical reason for not being able to learn. Their brain is injured or undeveloped. Some seem to choose to stop learning because they are afraid of change or are satisfied with life as it is. New information might challenge their ways, and they will not allow themselves to open their minds.

If we work in the clinical side of patient care, a closed mind can have particularly unfortunate consequences. It can result in significant medical errors. Every day, thousands of our patients entrust their lives to us. We cannot afford to become rigid in our thinking or negative in our attitudes. Our patients deserve more. Our calling requires more. There is no choice to be otherwise.

Today, for my personal growth and professional development, I will be open to new ideas and new information.

$\mathcal{A}$ Day of Profound Care

One day over sixty years ago, Russian Allied Forces opened the gates of Auschwitz and found more than seven thousand starving women and men. That day marked the end of one of the most infamous atrocities that man has perpetrated against man.

Take a moment during this workday to ponder the paraphrased sentiments of a survivor:

God was absent; neither felt nor seen. What I have learned from Auschwitz is that you and I, as well as every single human being, must now do what God would have done if he were there ... and would do if he were here ... that is, to turn toward one another in infinitely caring ways.

"To do what God would have done if he were there" are words of a man with profound faith. We can let them become our words by turning toward our patients, colleagues, strangers, and loved ones with profound care and human compassion.

I will observe the depth of caring taking place all around me and seek to support that. I am grateful for the skill of my colleagues and everyone who participates in the healing and caring that is taking place here.

Going Beyond Your Job Description

Have you recognized how we sometimes go through life as if asleep and then we're shocked into awareness by an unexpected event? That happened to me recently.

Last week, I had bilateral upper lid blepharoplasty surgery to correct a drooping eyelid. While lying on the operating table before the procedure, a nurse asked me if I was comfortable. I said, "Sort of, but I'm cold." In a matter of seconds, a warm blanket appeared! "Anything else?" "Nope, I feel fine." Within a few minutes when everything was ready, the anesthesiologist placed a plastic mask over my nose and mouth and said, "The mask will smell a little like plastic. We're ready to start the oxygen. Soon you will be asleep." Standard procedure.

What happened next was not. The nurse asked me again if I was comfortable. I nodded, yet I wasn't telling the whole truth. I did not tell her that I was actually thinking that I could die during this procedure. People sometimes do. After a moment the nurse leaned over and said, "I'll be here all during the procedure. I won't leave you." She placed her hand on my shoulder and I felt as secure as I have ever felt. I remember thinking that—even if I did not wake up—everything was okay. It was her touch that awakened as well as healed.

Why do I tell you this story? Because it taught me afresh what everyone in our field knows, yet is easily lost: when we extend ourselves beyond what is minimally required, we ourselves are rewarded. As nurses, doctors and others who are directly responsible for patient care, we are invited on a daily basis to touch our fellow human beings in a moving way, one that is so profound that it is transforming. No job description can adequately describe the sense of honor of being in the position of influencing another vulnerable human being.

A "job" becomes a "calling" when we follow our intuition and anticipate and wordlessly meet another person's needs, when we hold the hand of a scared patient, or stroke her hair, or give her a warm blanket and squeeze her hand. The reward, if we need one, comes as we experience that moment of being present to the other person. Being present is a gift to the patient as well as to ourselves. When we extend ourselves to others, we too, are deeply changed. Few other human experiences rival this moment in its beauty and value.

All of us are not nurses, chaplains or physicians. Many are electricians, office assistants, techs, nutritionists, carpenters, executives, accountants, and housekeepers. In our day-to-day work, these deeply moving experiences with others are not as likely to happen. However, opportunities will still arise with coworkers that are perhaps not as dramatic.

Whatever our jobs, we have an opportunity to be a supportive presence to others. The encounter might occur in the hallway, in a meeting, or on the phone. We can prepare ourselves by quietly seeking the courage to speak with others when we sense their need.

Today, I will make a conscious decision to offer reassurance to someone. If I need that reassurance today, I will be open to receiving it. I will perpetuate a circle of caring.

$\mathcal{M}$aking Decisions

Sometimes, I live as if decisions come easily to me. After all, I tell myself, I am the leader, and I can't appear unknowing by asking for advice. I also don't want to risk receiving advice that I don't agree with, and then not follow the recommendation I sought. There are hundreds of reasons to make decisions all by myself—and all of them are wrong. On decisions, Walt Whitman said, "When all men think alike, very little is thought of." As a thought group of one, how many diverse opinions can you have?

It has taken a long time to learn how important it is to surround myself with people who are willing to risk expressing different perspectives and alternatives. They are equally important as contrarians. I call them my "spotters," another word for supporters. My team expects me to make decisions when they need to be made and also to facilitate a process that includes them in my thinking. I count on them to help me make informed decisions.

Every day, each of us faces difficult decisions. Every time we make one, we are influencing someone else's world. That alone makes us leaders. When we need to make tough decisions, who are our "spotters"? Who will share their thinking and give us a different perspective? At times, we may feel alone and that there is no one we can trust. Speaking from experience, I can tell you this is an illusion.

Confide in people. The isolation we sometimes feel is of our own making. With a team that "spots," decisions are opportunities not only to promote patient care, but to mature personally and professionally.

Today, I will look for a team I can trust to provide different perspectives. I will try not to go it alone in my decision-making.

Being Connected

Here are some examples of employees caring for one another:

Yesterday, while cleaning a patient's room, one of our employees died. Two patients witnessed his death, and an observer described what followed. "You couldn't believe how the staff responded. They seemed to react as one person. Their emotions were so singularly in tune with one another that words were unnecessary. When they saw a need, they just took it upon themselves to do what needed to be done. No one person stood out. It seemed as if they had rehearsed their "dance."

A year ago, an environmental service employee had a serious motorcycle accident. During his recuperation, he ran out of earned vacation time. Other employees donated theirs, not an easy thing when work already takes up such a huge chunk of their lives. I saw the man the other day. He was all smiles. Even though he will never know all the people who dedicated their time, he was clearly grateful. Is it unusual that all these people would sacrifice themselves just for a coworker? Not at all. It is one more example of what we do when we feel connected one to another.

One day, a physician, on his way from the pharmacy to the floor, passed a woman who was clearly lost and late for an appointment. When the doctor asked her where she wanted to go, the physician discovered that it was to an office in an adjacent building. He actually accompanied the patient to that office just because she needed him to. Couldn't be, you might say. Physicians don't have that kind of time. But, the story is true.

And how about the nurse who changed the days she worked to accommodate a colleague who wanted to be home when her child returned from his first day at school? A small thing? Not to the child; neither to his mother.

These are everyday occurrences brought about by ordinary professionals. Our offices are more than buildings. They are places where we love in particularly unique ways.

If I see an opportunity to help today, I will offer my time, talent or services in whatever way possible. I will be changed for the better and so will the other person.

Honoring Unique Gifts

Rosh Hashanah began yesterday. This two-day celebration marks the beginning of the Jewish New Year. It is the time when our colleagues think of G-d as opening the Book of Life, observing all creatures, and giving them the opportunity to adjust their ways.

Jewish families relish this holiday and the coming series of holy days that follow. This season will be marked by family gatherings, special foods, and deeply felt memories of those who died, particularly parents and family members. There is a unique depth and quietness about this holiday.

Many of our employees are of the Jewish faith. Each is a gift just as every one of us is a gift. One of our strengths lies in the fact that we are remarkably diverse in race, ethnicity, religion and education. Without that diversity, we would never be able to understand, respect and serve our patients who have equally diverse backgrounds. Precisely because we want to serve our patients in the best ways possible, we need to recognize our differences. Our mission unites us; our individual talents and differences bring new life to our work.

Today, our Jewish colleagues have drawn apart to be with their families. When they return to work after the holidays, let's look for opportunities to express our appreciation to them for reminding us of the unique gifts that they, and each of us, bring to our patients.

What unique gifts and perspective do I bring to the work place? What is unique about my colleagues? My respect for others will grow as I learn more about other traditions.

$\mathcal{T}$he Tradition of the Holidays
in the Hospital

In many ways, the modern work place makes the story behind Christmas day seem part of a distant past. With the donkeys and the hay and the frankincense and myrrh, it's hard to bring the relevance of the birth of Jesus into today's world. Yet the underlying meaning of the holiday is not distant. It is another way of acknowledging and celebrating the holiness imbedded within the human heart and the sacredness of the home we call earth. Hanukkah has a similar message of rededication of spirit and the expression of spiritual values in the everyday experience. This understanding of the world is something all of us can share, whatever our traditions and cultures.

In spite of the spiritual underpinning of this special day, we still have jobs to do. Many employees have to work during the holidays so that thousands of patients can receive the care they need. Hospital rooms must be cleaned, nourishment provided, faucets repaired, diagnoses made, and medicines prescribed. The care on a holiday is as good as it is on any other day. The only way this can happen is because of the selflessness of caregivers. Their goodness and generosity are easily overlooked.

On Christmas day, you can walk into any hospital and everything will seem quite ordinary. Staff is going about their business taking care of patients. Yet, the fact that these workers are there is what makes it so wondrous. Their care on this day is a way of making kindness tangible. These acts are rumors of sacredness. To those who work on holidays, thank you.

I am grateful for the opportunity to work with a dedicated team of people. I will be an expression of healing and caring, remembering why I chose this work.

ℬeing Present

Another employee and I were invited to speak at a community center on the topic of end-of-life care. The room was packed with elderly residents of a nearby high-rise retirement home. Our talk focused on aging with dignity and the need for Advanced Directives. We were explaining to the audience the "Five Wishes" document that helps people prepare for such moments.

As I sat and watched my colleague make her presentation, it was clear she had everyone's attention. You could have heard a pin drop in the room. It turned out that her interest in the topic came from an intensely personal experience when her husband of two years unexpectedly fell ill and died within six months. She spoke about how difficult it was for her to prepare for the death of her young husband. Afterward, she explained how to complete the Advanced Directive document.

Why was she communicating so well? Many would say it was because the subject was so pertinent to this audience. It could also have been her solid grasp of the subject matter and her uncanny ability to be funny while speaking on a difficult topic. It was clear to me, however, that her ability to engage the audience came from her willingness to reveal something about herself. This invited the audience's trust. She risked being exposed. The risk was rewarded. She created a connection and built a bond of closeness as the audience heard her story.

We are highly trained, competent professionals. Whether our jobs are maintaining buildings, preparing food, typing letters, nursing at the bedside, reviewing charts, running tests, prescribing meds, operating on patients or simply visiting them, we have the opportunity to be a healing presence. Technical competence is never an obstacle to being a healing presence. The challenge is to put more of *us* into our actions, to bring that rare and magical quality called presence into every moment of the day.

"Presence" is more than just a basic awareness of the physical details around us. It is the best of us that is available and ready to "come out" any time. We become present when we invite our authentic core to come to the surface.

Being present involves a choice. We can choose to operate like a robot or we can take the risk to allow the full expression of our unique selves to shine through our actions, words and attitudes throughout the day.

Those few words, *being present where we are*, are extremely important. They describe a person who is engaged.

I will invite all of who I am—my training, my experience, and yes, even my authentic core—to the task at hand. I will see how this enriches my life and adds to others' experience.

Honoring Those
Who Came Before Us

Labor Day is rooted in the history of the American laborer who toiled under the weight of tedious, backbreaking work. Unionization paved the way for the rights and protections we take for granted today: the 8-hour workday, the 5-day work week, paid vacations, and safety protection. This legal holiday is one way to acknowledge the power and value of those who fought for their rights so we could have ours.

We are a privileged people. We have time and a life apart from work, which many in the world do not have. We have time to reflect. Who is not grateful?

Long weekends open a space in the normal pattern of our workaday lives. We have time to reflect on the ways in which we are blessed. Our good fortune rests on the efforts of those who have gone before us as well as those who work beside us.

While it may be difficult to express our gratitude to those whose contribution was made in the distant past, we can nevertheless express to others, patients, our loved ones, and colleagues, how much we appreciate them.

Today, I will find a way to show appreciation for my coworkers. I will express my gratitude for all the ways they help me improve the work I do.

Valuing Partnership, Celebrating Competition

Within the clinical world, we think in terms of "diagnoses." An accurate diagnosis helps us understand an illness and guides us as we develop the appropriate plan of care. While we usually think of diagnoses in terms of individuals, it is also a way to understand organizations.

During a meeting at one of our hospitals attended mostly by managers and directors, it was announced that patient satisfaction with their care had risen significantly. The room broke into a spontaneous ovation. A sense of pride was undeniable. Collectively, we felt rewarded for the conscious effort we had made to be more aware of patient needs.

After making the announcement, the CEO acknowledged how good it felt and how proud he was of our progress. Then he added, "We are pleased, as we should be, with our results. However, remember that our colleagues (the sister hospitals within the system that did not significantly improve) are working equally hard to improve their scores. Let's find ways to celebrate, not as winners, but as colleagues." He was aware that while a competitive environment can motivate, it can also have an adverse effect. If a hospital were to flaunt its accomplishments, collaboration and teamwork would be stymied. One-upsmanship does not create cultures that support healing, teamwork, and partnership.

The next day, I attended a weekly meeting of managers and directors at one of those sister hospitals. The CEO announced the success of their sister hospital. There was unprompted applause. They were genuinely supportive and appreciative of their colleagues' accomplishments.

The diagnosis? Their organization is healthy. What was the symptom leading to the diagnosis? They were able to genuinely enjoy another's success without feeling that this success was their loss.

The only way to provide the very best patient care is to recognize that each of us on every team affects the quality of this care. We are interconnected. Celebrating the success of one team is cause for all of us to celebrate. Honoring and acknowledging the value that all of us contribute to an organization enhances our work and the quality of care we bring to all of our patients. If we have a real passion for improving patient care, we understand the importance of valuing every team's contribution and the value of every member on every team. We can work together as a team to celebrate what we, and others in our organization have accomplished. It is up to us—not just others—to find creative and life-giving ways to celebrate. At its best, health care is built on the value of partnering, not competition.

I will recognize the value that every member of every team brings to my organization.

Being More Than What We Do

We are a combination of what we do and who we are. Being and doing are two sides of the same coin. We need both. If we believe we are fine just the way we are and do not have to do anything, we are mistaken. If we think "doing" is the only thing that is important, that is equally limiting and short-sighted. The quality of what we do is as important as what we do or how much we do.

When we accent *being* at the expense of *doing*, we become ineffective. When we focus on *doing* at the expense of *being*, work loses its inspiration. We overlook the value of expressing human qualities in our work, and work becomes drudgery.

Almost everyone craves a work place where they are valued both for what they do and who they are. It is up to us to create the climate.

Today, I will be a human being and a human doing. There is a place for both parts of me. I will notice and acknowledge my coworkers as human *be*ings.

*H*onoring the Beauty and Sacredness of Our Surroundings

Today is Earth Day, marked by celebrations, tree plantings, speeches, and mobilized groups promoting open space, the cleaning of our streets and the painting of homes in low-income areas. It reminds us that you and I are entrusted with the care of this world. Someone who sees the world as a garden lives in a different world than one who thinks of the earth as raw material. Someone who sees the earth as a garden will treat it with love and respect, will recognize its seasons, and will help it grow. A person who sees it as his own personal garbage dump takes what he wants from it and throws away whatever he wants, regardless of the consequences.

Today, the sky is cloudless, the air is dry, and the temperature warm. Yet most of us will not see the day's beauty nor feel its warmth. We live in windowless operating rooms, business offices, and surgery centers. We come to work before seven and leave when only an hour or two of light remains. The world that has been entrusted to our care during the work week is indoors, yet it is no less sacred.

Earth Day gives us a chance to pause and think about our environment. When we have perspective, these patient-centered, windowless worlds of hospitals and offices can become as beautiful as the mountains and plains that surround the cities. Each of us can create a garden within the work place by shaping how we work with our colleagues and how we serve those entrusted to our care. The challenge here is to remember that we co-create the world in which we live.

Today, I will do one small thing to make my world more beautiful. I will look for the beauty in my work environment and treat it as sacred.

The Spiritual Side of Health Care

Medical residents meet every morning to discuss various medical issues with their physician teachers. Recently, I sat among the ninety resident docs. The topic focused on the residency training experience: what areas of medical practice were emphasized, the expectations that were placed on residents, and residents' experience as new doctors. One of the physicians asked the residents, "In your program, is attention paid to your spiritual care and that of your patients?" The physicians all chuckled uncomfortably at the question.

While I left the meeting wondering why they laughed, I had a hunch. Physicians have told me that as they go through medical school and gain an understanding of how the body works, they leave with a wealth of knowledge about the body and a lost sense of the spiritual side of life. This is unfortunate because when a physician enters a patient's room, that person is looking for a physician-healer.

What do we mean by spiritual? Many think the word is a reference to piety, involvement with a faith community or with a belief system. Spirituality is something more.

When a resident is asked to consider a patient's spiritual needs, she must ask herself, "Can I be a healer?" That is an unsettling question. Who would not draw back when asked? She may feel unequal to the task and perhaps inadequately prepared to meet this expectation. If we look more closely at what we mean by tending to a patient's spiritual or emotional needs, our resident may feel more confident in her ability to "heal" a patient in this way. We do this by being attuned to their needs as human beings and responding with heart. This allows us to provide a deeper level of care that supports the medical treatment they are receiving.

The spiritual side of life is always present. We are more than our physicality. The spiritual side of life is embedded within, and not separate from, the ordinariness of everyday life. We are wholly body and wholly spirit. We are never only body or only spirit. If we are uncomfortable talking about this side of life, we need to ask ourselves why. To be an effective healer we cannot be fearful or unfamiliar with this side of life.

I will be open to the physical and spiritual sides of life. I am a better healer when I embrace and acknowledge both.

Awakening to the Sacredness of Life–and Our Work

Most days seem ordinary. We have the responsibilities that go along with managing a household, raising children and holding down a job. Before arriving at work, we have to prepare lunches and get our children off to school (or at least out of bed). We may not even have time for a bowl of cereal, a piece of toast or a cup of coffee. If we're really lucky, we may have time to exercise a little before climbing into our car to make our way to work.

Every once in a while we are shocked into a more reflective place when our taken-for-granted world is disrupted. Tragedy can do that. So can love. Both can awaken us to the sacredness of our work and world.

Once we find a moment to retreat from the distractions, we can become consciously aware of the sacredness of the work we do, right down to the tiniest task. Just because something is ordinary doesn't mean it isn't sacred.

Today, I will shake myself awake. I have opportunities to care.

Index by Topic

RESPECTING AND VALUING OUR COLLEAGUES

BEING AUTHENTIC AT WORK

About the Authors

MARTIN HELLDORFER, D. MINISTRY

 The primary author of *Healing with Heart*, Dr. Martin C. Helldorfer, has the kind of education and work experience that not only qualifies him to write this book, it has inspired him to write it.

Martin is currently the Senior Vice President for Mission at Exempla Healthcare, a Colorado based regional health care system. Prior to joining Exempla, he served in similar positions, and as Senior Vice President for Human Resources in other regional and national health care systems—serving on Boards and often as an organization's ethical and spiritual advisor. He is intimately familiar with the inner workings of health care organizations.

Martin's experience working with employees within hospitals is extensive. He worked for twenty years as a psychologist working within two specialized psychiatric residential treatment centers for professionals.

His two books, stemming from his clinical work, *The Work Trap*, and *Prayer, A Guide When Troubled*, were in continuous print for fifteen years.

He holds a Doctorate in psychology (Andover Newton Theological) and masters degrees in chemistry (Notre Dame University), religion and personality (Duquesne University) and theology (La Salle University).

Dr. Helldorfer was a monk (De La Salle Brothers) for more than thirty years. His background is rich; his words both challenging and affirming. He lives with his wife in the Denver, Colorado area.

TERRI MOSS

Terri Moss is an employee and marketing communications consultant with 26 years of experience. She has worked for several of the premier human resources consulting firms in the country, as well as for a behavioral health care medical facility, and presently runs her own consulting firm and publishing house, Moss Communications. Her clients include Fortune 100 companies representing the high tech, health care, public utilities, finance and retail industries.

Her work experience has given her a unique understanding of the particular challenges and stresses that health care professionals face. Through her work and her extensive experience as a hospital volunteer, she has developed a deep sensitivity to their particular challenges and the environment in which they work. Her inspiration to pursue the writing and publication of *Healing With Heart* comes from her deep commitment to, and appreciation for the importance of clear communication among employees and throughout an organization.

Terri has a long-held mission to create practical, everyday work tools to help employees achieve a renewed attitude for their work; one that is inspired and personally fulfilling. Terri has been an avid and devoted meditator for 29 years. She lives with her husband, inspiring son and wonder-dog and Therapy Pet, Cody, in the San Francisco Bay Area.